Twayne's United States Authors Series

Sylvia E. Bowman, *Editor*

INDIANA UNIVERSITY

Josh Billings
(Henry Wheeler Shaw)

Josh Billings
(Henry Wheeler Shaw)

By DAVID B. KESTERSON
North Texas State University

 **229**

Twayne Publishers, Inc. :: New York

PS
2808
.K4

ISBN 0-8057-0058-7

MANUFACTURED IN THE UNITED STATES OF AMERICA

To Linda, Todd, and Chad

Preface

I FIRST became interested in Henry Wheeler Shaw because of the distinct differences between his writings and those of his fellow literary comedians. Indeed, the misspellings of Charles Farrar Browne (Artemus Ward) are present, but Browne's narrations and dramatic situations are not; nor are the political-social concerns so significant in the works of David Ross Locke (Petroleum V. Nasby). Shaw concentrated on the modes of the aphorism, the familiar essay, and the sketch. Economy of wording and a certain classic balance of language are his fortes. Most prominent among the differences between Shaw and his contemporary humorists, however, is the fact that Shaw's "Josh Billings" is not really a persona in the fashion of Browne's "Artemus Ward" or Locke's "Petroleum V. Nasby." Billings is rarely a separate person from Shaw; he remains the pseudonym rather than the persona, a fact that relates him more to Mark Twain than to either Nasby or Ward. Whenever we read Josh Billings, we are listening to Shaw, who is genuine, unassuming, and wise in his humorous manner.

The surprising thing about Henry Wheeler Shaw is his modernity—in tone as well as in much of his subject matter. The cacography recedes into the background the more Shaw is read; and his wit, common sense, and keen perceptions of life emerge to the forefront. His originality is always striking. It takes only one such saying as "When a feller gits a goin down hil, it dus seem as tho evry thing had bin greased for the okashun" for the reader to forget the quaint language and settle down to the enjoyment of a lively wit.

In this book I have undertaken to study Shaw both as a humorist in the crackerbox tradition to which he and many of his contemporaries partially belonged and as an individual, humorous philosopher working in his own vein. I have emphasized his accomplishments in the aphorism and the essay, the two forms most compatible with his method of thinking and writing. But his other accomplishments are also treated in detail: his miscellaneous short pieces, his jest books, his satirical *Farmer's Allminax* (the work which gave him the most fame), and his highly successful lecturing. Finally, I have traced close to a century of critical reaction to Shaw, a survey that leads to recent new departures in reevaluating his contributions.

The text of Shaw's works presents something of a problem. Most of his essays and aphorisms appeared originally in the *New York Weekly* over the eighteen years he actively wrote for it. The files of the *Weekly*, however, are both incomplete and generally inaccessible; therefore, the general reader and the scholar are usually forced to consult the published volumes of Shaw's works for reading or reference. Thus, with a few exceptions, I have used the published books as my sources rather than the *Weekly*. Even at that, I have quoted liberally from these works since they are out of print and since many of them are not commonly found in libraries.

In writing this volume, I have incurred numerous debts that I now gratefully acknowledge. I have relied on the staffs of many libraries to make some of Shaw's works and much obscure critical material available to me. I am particularly indebted to the state libraries of Maine and Connecticut; the public libraries of Boston and New York; the Hamilton College Library; and the university libraries of Chicago, Harvard, Illinois, Texas, Yale, and Wyoming. Certainly my major debt in this line, however, is to the fine staff of the North Texas State University Library, especially Mr. John W. Brewster and Miss Ellie N. Whitmore.

A number of individuals provided assistance and inspiration: Professor Ray Lewis White of Illinois State University; Mrs. Charles Glasgow of Denton, Texas; my colleagues in the English Department at North Texas State University; the members of the Faculty Research Committee at North Texas State University who made possible time and money for research and writing; Mr. Homer R. Kesterson of the University of Wyoming; Professor Frederick Anderson, Editor of the Mark Twain Papers at the University of California, Berkeley; Mr. Cyril Clemens of Webster

Preface

Groves, Missouri; Research assistants Mrs. Karleen Barlow, Mrs. Diane Oliver Taylor, and Miss Carolyn Collinsworth; and my wife Linda, who provided dutiful editing and proofreading along with abundant patience. Above all, I am deeply indebted to Professor Joseph Jones of the University of Texas at Austin for his spontaneous, enthusiastic, and totally unselfish aid in sharing with me some of his own insights, Billingsiana, and notes. I hope I can repay some of my debt to him by doing justice in this volume to the humorist we both enjoy and admire. To all of the above-named individuals—and to others who have given encouragement and expressed interest along the way—I am grateful.

DAVID B. KESTERSON

North Texas State University
Denton

Contents

Chronology

1818 Henry Wheeler Shaw born, April 21, in Lanesboro, Massachusetts.

1833 Entered Hamilton College in Utica, New York.

1834 Expelled from Hamilton College during sophomore year.

1835 Went West; traveled and worked (mainly in the Middle West) until 1845.

1845 Returned to Lanesboro. Marriage to Zilpha Bradford, February 18, followed by nine years of moving about and working at different jobs. Two daughters born during these years.

1854 The Shaws settled in Poughkeepsie, New York. Shaw worked as auctioneer and realtor. In December, bought and operated for six months an Ohio River steamboat, the *Hurricane.*

1858 Elected Alderman in Poughkeepsie, representing fourth ward. Probably began during this year to submit humorous articles to the *New Ashford Eagle* under the pen name Ephrem Billings.

1859 Began contributing epigrams and essays to the Poughkeepsie *Daily Press* and the weekly *Poughkeepsian,* first using pseudonym of Si Sledlength (shortly changed to Josh Billings).

1863 Began lecturing. For several years had little success. Then became popular. Lectured for approximately twenty years.

1865 *Josh Billings, Hiz Sayings,* Shaw's first book published with the aid of Artemus Ward.

1866? In this year or the next, Shaws moved to New York City.

1867 Shaw began his long-lived career as columnist on the *New York Weekly* beginning May 30.

1868 *Josh Billings on Ice, and Other Things,* Shaw's second book.

1869 The first installment of *Josh Billings' Farmer's Allminax,* which was to run through 1880. Engaged by James C. Redpath to lecture under the auspices of the famous Boston Lyceum Bureau.

1873 Published *Twelve Ansestrals Sighns in the Billings' Zodiac Gallery,* a reprint of the *Farmer's Allminax* for 1874.

1874 Highly successful lecture trip across country to West coast. Publication of *Everybody's Friend, or Josh Billings' Encyclopoedia and Proverbial Philosophy of Wit and Humor,* a collection of almost everything Shaw had written to date. First number of *Josh Billings' Spice Box* published.

1876 *Complete Comical Writings of Josh Billings* appeared.

1877 The jest book *Josh Billings' Trump Kards* published.

1879 Ten years of the *Farmer's Allminax* collected in *Old Probability: Perhaps Rain—Perhaps Not*, Shaw's favorite book.

1880 *Josh Billings' Cook Book and Picktorial Proverbs* appeared.

1881 Published *Josh Billings Struggling with Things*.

1884 In March, began "Uncle Esek's Wisdom," a column for the *Century Magazine*, which ran until September, 1888.

1885 In August, journeyed to West Coast for health and rest. Died October 14 in Monterey, California.

1888 *The Complete Works of Josh Billings* published.

1902 *Josh Billings' Old Farmer's Allminax, 1870-1879*, appeared.

I pin all my faith, hope, and charity upon this one impulse of my nature, and that is, if I could have my way, there would be a smile continually on the face of every human being on God's footstool, and this smile should ever and anon widen into a broad grin.—Josh Billings

CHAPTER 1

Man of Many Trades

N OT until 1870, when Henry Wheeler Shaw was fifty-two, did he as Josh Billings win national fame in all facets of his literary career as a comic lecturer, a literary wit, a burlesque almanac writer, and a grass-roots philosopher. Taking up the pen seriously when he was in his middle forties, Shaw brought to his writings a background that encompassed years of such varied formative experiences as farming, auctioneering, steamboating, politicking, pioneering, and selling real estate. Because of the adventures of his first forty years, he developed a broad range of interests and a keen perception of human nature. His "education" in the school of life began in a modest New England village whose denizens embodied the kind of earnestness, moral fiber, and philosophical outlook on life that heavily influenced him and became the bases of his literary subject matter.

I *Background and Youth*

Shaw was born on April 21, 1818, in the Berkshire hills so loved by Nathaniel Hawthorne and Herman Melville. His birthplace of Lanesboro was a small, homey, yet enterprising little town. As young Henry grew up, he was presented with ideal natural scenery for enjoyment and with the prosperous lives of hard-working, frugal people for instruction. Lanesboro boasted five hotels, three tanneries, two cloth-dressing factories, numerous gristmills and stores. Large quantities of marble were exported from its quarries to other parts of the country. Only after mid-century, when railroads favored more conveniently located neighboring towns, did the little burg lose importance and slip quietly into the role of a sleepy farming community.[1]

Shaw's family was a prosperous, enlightened, active one. Several were involved in politics. His paternal grandfather, Dr. Samuel Shaw, a successful Vermont physician and surgeon, was for a number of years a United States congressman from Rutland County, Vermont. John Savage, Shaw's maternal uncle, was chief justice of the state of New York for many years. Shaw's own father, Henry Shaw, took an extremely active part in politics: in 1820, when he was only twenty-four years old, he was elected to Congress from the Berkshire County district, and he was a member of the Massachusetts senate and legislature for twenty-five years. He was a close friend of Henry Clay, and he managed Clay's political career in New England from 1816 to 1840.[2] Young Henry's mother, Laura Wheeler Shaw, came from a prosperous farm family of Lanesboro. She was evidently a woman who possessed both good sense and charm.

Despite the relatively sobering New England environment, Shaw as a youth was extremely restless; he was inclined to be prankish and unscholarly. But he displayed early the good nature that he was fortunate to have all his life, and he exhibited a fresh enthusiasm and keen curiosity about life—traits that led him into many disparate adventures.

His schooling was ordinary. He first attended a district school; then, for college preparation, enrolled in an academy at nearby Lenox where he learned what he was to acquire of Latin and Greek from John Hotchin, a dedicated teacher and Classicist. Shaw, who profited from the guidance and strict academic regimen of Hotchin, years later remembered the old master's admonition to his pupils: "Whatever you get, get it got."[3] In all his formal schooling—even including college—Shaw "got" more under Professor Hotchin than from anyone else. The academy proved to be, therefore, his most significant formal educational experience.

In 1833, when Shaw was fifteen years old, he entered Hamilton College, a Presbyterian school in Clinton, New York. Caring little for his formal studies, he engaged in numerous other activities. He made many friends, enjoyed taking extensive nature walks into the surrounding area, and indulged in his share of college-boy pranks. One stunt led to his expulsion during his sophomore year—climbing a lightning rod and removing the clapper from the chapel bell. Even though he was expelled,

Shaw was so popular among his classmates that he infected the majority of the boys with the craze for climbing the lightning rod. The ascent was so dangerous, since the rod bent under and around a protruding cornice, that the faculty eventually had long spikes installed in the cornice close to the rod to ward off climbers. In honor of Shaw's maiden ascent, these spikes became known as "'Josh Billings' spikes."[4]

Though Shaw, in leaving formal schooling forever, took little with him academically, he had learned much about life. As Cyril Clemens has said, "He began to exercise that gift for character analysis that later on made it possible for him to produce such shrewd observations."[5]

II   *"Go West, Young Man"*

When Shaw was returning to Hamilton for his sophomore year, he met several adventurers just back from the far West with stories that excited his already vivid and restless imagination. After he was expelled later that year, he returned to Lanesboro, read Shakespeare, and dreamed of going West. His father finally consented to Henry's stubborn wishes, gave him ten dollars, and sent him on his way. Shaw was seventeen.

Records for Shaw's ten adventuresome years, 1835-45, spent in the West are unfortunately scanty. It is known that he had used up all his money by the time he got to Illinois, that he sojourned a while in Saint Louis, and that he met there a group of youths who were planning an expedition to the West. Shaw promptly joined the venture and was elected leader. Their goal—an impossible one for amateurs—was to reach the Rocky Mountains via Missouri, Kansas, and Nebraska and to explore the South Pass region, a challenge only to be met years later by General John Frémont. But Shaw—optimistic and bolstered by letters of introduction from family friends John Quincy Adams, Henry Clary, and Martin Van Buren—set out to find the golden West. On the plains of Kansas, however, the golden West lost its glitter as illness set in, a young geologist in the party died, food grew scarce, and hostile Indians threatened. Back to Saint Louis, then, trudged the disappointed party, leaving the West to Frémont and others more prepared for the customary hazards.

Shaw's spirit of adventure was undaunted, however. After stopping in Saint Louis, he departed for Toledo, Ohio; met two adventure-hungry friends, Gideon Weed and Josh Carew; and set out with them up the Maumee River, ending up penniless in Napoleon, Indiana. To extricate themselves from poverty, the three dreamed up a public performance, a lecture on mesmerism to be delivered by Shaw and some humorous songs to be offered by Carew. Shaw—for the first time taking the platform that over thirty years later would make him nationally known—posed as "Mordecai David," descendant of the biblical David; and he read his lecture to an enthusiastic audience. The three friends were such a success that night in Napoleon that they took their show to surrounding towns.

One other interlude from this otherwise rather vague ten-year period is known. Shaw spent about a year (date uncertain) in Norwalk, Ohio, where he worked a few weeks in a law office; engaged in some sport against a congregation of Millerites; and, as a ruse, delivered a lecture on "Milk" (during which—when being interrupted and asked why he was saying nothing on milk— he replied, " 'Not lecturing *on* milk? Why, I drank a quart of milk before I mounted the platform. Of course, I have been lecturing *on* milk.' "[6] Shaw sent his audience home laughing. Interestingly enough, when he later turned professional lecturer, he used the title "Milk" for one of the main lectures in his repertoire.

III   *The Settled Life?*

In 1845, now twenty-seven years old, Shaw returned to Lanes-boro where on February 18 he married his childhood sweetheart Zilpha Bradford of Lanesboro, a descendant of William Brad-ford, the colonial governor of Plymouth. The wedding was solemnized in nearby Lebanon, New York, in order to avoid the waiting period in Massachusetts caused by the required reading of banns and also probably to escape retaliation from young married friends whom the mischievous Shaw had harassed at their weddings.

The newly married couple settled in Lanesboro for a few

years, where Henry tried farming; then, in typical Shaw fashion, they took to the road. They traveled in the West where Shaw farmed; they sojourned in Virginia where he opened a coal mine; and they settled briefly in Saratoga, New York, where they decided to educate the two daughters of whom they had become proud parents. Shaw's daughters were additions to his life that brought him as much delight as had marriage itself. His later essays and sayings show him to have been a dedicated husband and family man.

Like the period of Shaw's earlier travels in the West, the years 1846-54 are hazy. But in 1854 Shaw settled his family in Poughkeepsie, New York, which was to be home for many years. In an office within sight of his house, the thirty-six-year-old Shaw advertised himself as an auctioneer and real-estate agent; and he soon found success in both roles. After a few months in operation, he once more set aside his business to snatch another opportunity that promised financial success—operating a steamboat on the Ohio River. After Christmas, 1854, he went to Pittsburgh, bought the *Hurricane*, and attempted to establish a successful run. The severity of wintry Ohio weather, however, both hampered river travel and harassed the crew. By spring, Shaw was weary of the boatman's life;[7] he sold the *Hurricane* on July 27 and returned to Poughkeepsie to enjoy a quieter existence.

That quieter life in Poughkeepsie was to bring him a large measure of satisfaction and cause him to involve himself in civic interests. He became one of the city's leading realtors and auctioneers;[8] he was elected to the city council in 1858; and he served as an active alderman who assisted in planning community activities such as the Poughkeepsie regatta and accompanying festivities.[9] He even became a charter member of the Poughkeepsie Baseball Club when it was organized in 1859. It was an amateur athletic club to which the members paid fees and dues; fun was the order of the day.[10] So comfortable did Shaw become in his new surroundings that he was on the verge of becoming merely another solid citizen, civic-minded and somewhat complacent. But a staid life for him was not in the offing.

IV   *Enter Josh Billings*

To while away the hours not involved in selling real estate or
auctioneering, Shaw began about 1859 to write humorous
sketches, a type of writing much in vogue at the time. Augustus
Baldwin Longstreet's *Georgia Scenes* [1835], Seba Smith's Jack
Downing letters [1830-54], and James Russell Lowell's *Biglow
Papers* [first series—1848]. Encouraged by friends, Shaw started
sending some of the pieces to the *New Ashford Eagle,* a small-
town newspaper in Massachusetts, under the name Efrem Billings. Both the pseudonym and the fact that the works were
published so far from Poughkeepsie were perhaps, as Cyril
Clemens suggests, a means of protecting his business success
since he was uncertain what effect being known as a writer would
have on his business.[11] But of course the use of the pseudonym
and persona had long been accepted fare among American
comic writers (Poor Richard, Hosea Biglow, Jack Downing,
Sam Slick), and Shaw was following suit. The letters Shaw wrote
to the *Eagle* were in dialect (another current style), and they
reported on the doings of a mythical rural community. Shades
of Lowell were certainly present.

The more Shaw wrote, the more confident he grew, and
eventually he was proud enough of his pieces to want them
published in more important newspapers as well as in papers
close to home. Thus he began contributing to the *Poughkeepsian*
and the *Poughkeepsie Daily Press*; he changed his pen name to
Si Sledlength; and he discarded the eccentric spelling in order
to make his works more suitable to urban readers.[12] Very soon,
however, he became dissatisfied both with his new name and with
the limited circulation of his writings; and he changed both.
His former adventurer friend, Josh Carew, had died recently;
Shaw liked the name, even contemplated adopting both first
and last names of his friend, and finally decided that Josh went
well with Billings, his first nom de plume. The name stuck, of
course, and became so widely known that throughout his career
Shaw's real name was not known by most people. In fact, Shaw
requested that Josh Billings be the name inscribed on his tomb-
stone.

The limited circulation problem, however, was more difficult to solve than the selection of a satisfactory pen name. Shaw wanted newspapers throughout the East to publish some of his pieces in their columns, but none of them seemed interested. He was dejected by such indifference to his submissions, and he was jolted when suddenly every major paper in the country printed an essay on the mule by Artemus Ward (Charles Farrar Browne) that was no better than—if as good as—the one he had written and published in the *Poughkeepsian*. The main difference between the two lay in style: Ward's was written in the quaint phonetic spellings characteristic of popular homespun humor of the time; Shaw's was not. Immediately correcting the matter, Shaw converted his "Essay on the Mule" to "Essa on the Muel, bi Josh Billings," and his name was made. A Boston newspaper bought the piece at once (at the humiliatingly low sum of $1.50), and three comic journals published it within a month—*Nick Nacks, Yankee Notions*, and *Budget of Phun*.[13] Despite the small financial reward, Shaw was so encouraged he started sending items steadily to various papers and magazines; and he received substantial remuneration for many of them. One of the more prestigious of his outlets was the *Sunday Mercury* (1838-90), a leading New York paper.[14]

In the same year (1864), Shaw contacted Artemus Ward for advice about publishing a book of witticisms and sketches. Ward responded enthusiastically; when the two men met in New York, Ward approved of the manuscript; and he urged his publisher and subsequently Shaw's—G. W. Carleton and Company—to publish it. Carleton did so in 1865 as *Josh Billings, Hiz Sayings*, and the book was highly successful. Josh Billings was launched, never again to want for literary fame. In the remaining twenty years of his life, Shaw published eight more volumes, wrote two major columns, and produced for ten years the famous *Josh Billings' Farmer's Allminax*.

V A New York Life

After the success of *Josh Billings, Hiz Sayings*, Shaw and his family moved to New York City, his residence for the rest of his life. New York, as Cyril Clemens has observed, "thrilled and delighted" Shaw. Not only was the city to provide ample profes-

sional opportunities as a writer, but nowhere else could Shaw
find a better laboratory for the study of human nature, a study
that, as Clemens says, "was at once his hobby and his profession."[15] In New York, the Shaws lived for the first few years in
an apartment across from Central Park; later, when Shaw grew
more affluent from his lecturing and almanac producing, the
family bought a house on Sixty-third Street. It was an unpre-
tentious abode with a garret which, as Will Clemens wrote,
was "made to answer the combined purpose of literary sanctum
and storehouse."[16] Shaw occupied two desks in New York—one
at Carleton's his publisher, and the other at the *New York
Weekly;* and, when not on the lecture circuit, he was usually in
one of the two places busily writing.

Probably the most important job Shaw had in his entire lifetime was his position as weekly columnist for the *New York
Weekly,* an appointment that began on May 30, 1867. The paper's
zealous owners, Francis S. Smith and Francis S. Street, proudly
announced in the *Weekly* for that day:

[Below we give No. 1. of a series of papers by the world-renowned
Josh Billings, who is now engaged to write exclusively for the *New
York Weekly.* Josh is now known wherever the English language
is spoken, and in some places where it is not. We, who have grown
familiar with his lucubrations, do not wonder at this, for the solid
chunks of wisdom which he dispenses are so well calculated to
benefit the human family, his ideas are so luminous, and his de-
ductions so clear, that "the wayfaring man, though a fool, need
not err therein." We bespeak for Josh Billings a host of new friends
among our readers, who will stick to him like a burr to a sheep's
wool. Let nobody, who is anybody, fail to read him.] (4)

Shaw's column, for which he received for every installment
a hundred dollars, appeared under general titles such as "The
Josh Billings' Papers," "Josh Billings' Spice Box," and "Josh
Billings' Philosophy"; but the composition of the column varied
from strings of aphorisms, to essays and sketches, to narratives,
to travel accounts. The material Shaw published in this column
comprises the bulk of his printed works, though much of it was
revised before appearing in book form.

Shaw was so popular with *Weekly* readers that he continued

under the employment of Street and Smith for the remaining eighteen years of his life. In fact, his column even appeared for several years posthumously; for Street and Smith had apparently decided not to announce Shaw's death. These co-owners, who tended to be overly enthusiastic about almost anything appearing in their paper, were especially proud of Shaw. They frequently ran blurbs about his *Allminax* and other published works, and they gave accounts of his lecture tours plus other bits of news about him—even family events such as the marriage of one of his daughters.[17] Typical of their boasts is the one Smith made in his biography of Shaw in 1883 that Shaw "has not written a line over the *nom de plume* of 'Josh Billings' for any other paper."[18]

Shaw may have been the "Exclusive" (as Street and Smith liked to call him) for the *Weekly*—at least under the name Josh Billings—but that fact did not keep other newspapers from pirating his columns, a practice that not only attested to Shaw's talent and popularity but also greatly irritated Street and Smith. In an effort to stop the wholesale borrowing, Shaw wrote the following "Hint to the Newspaper Publick" in the *Weekly* for April 15, 1869—an interesting reaction in that it lays as many compliments at the feet of the *Weekly*'s proprietors as it offers admonishments to the pirates (Shaw was always a good businessman). It is also written almost entirely in correct spelling, perhaps in order to make it more emphatic:

Dear Editors and Publishers: Thare iz nothing that fills my heart with more satisfaction and joy than to see my productions so universally copyed into the various journals, periodicals, daylies, weeklys, semi-weeklies, monthlys, railroad guides, almanacks and pattent medicine volumes of the day. It is an *evidence of good sense on the part of those who copy,* and certainly don't show a want of sense in the author.

Now, while this is so intensely flattering to me, it is not courtesy to my employers. I am engaged by the gentlemanly editors of the *New York Weekly* to write exclusively for their paper, which has a larger circulation than any other literary paper in the Union, and I am paid as much, according to the amount of matter furnished, as any other writer in America.

I don't think I have furnished the *New York Weekly* an article for the last two years that has not been copied into some other paper, and in no one single instance has credit been given to the *Weekly*.

Now, gentlemen, publishers and editors, is this strictly honorable? I know that you will answer *No*!

Let me hope that hereafter when you do me the honor to transfer my productions to your collums, you will do the *New York Weekly* the justice to credit them with the favor.

I don't make this appeal for the *Weekly* that the paper, pecuniarily, nor for reputation's sake, needs the literary thunder of any of its contributors, but I make it upon the broad and level ground of equity, of courtesy, and gentlemanly propriety which should exist, and does exist, among the profession as literally as among any other.

Most respectfully, gentlemen, I am your humble servant,

Josh Billings (4)

Shaw's other New York assignment, and his last, was not undertaken until March, 1884, when he began contributing aphorisms to the *Century Illustrated Monthly Magazine* under the pen name Uncle Esek. As with his *New York Weekly* fame, his "Uncle Esek's Wisdom" column became so popular that the column was continued until September, 1888, three years after Shaw's death. The aphorisms Shaw wrote under the pseudonym Uncle Esek were different from his usual utterances only in that they did not appear with the characteristic misspellings and ungrammatical constructions. William Webster Ellsworth, an officer in the Century Company, later recalled concerning Shaw's contributions that "These little aphorisms came to us about forty at a time, each one written in pencil on a separate slip of paper. They were chunks of real wisdom too."[19]

VI   *The Man and His Friends*

The fact that Shaw was unusually perceptive of human nature made his homespun aphorisms, essays, and speeches particularly poignant and popular. Undoubtedly enhancing his success as a public figure, however, was an engaging personality and an urbane, basically mellow outlook on life.

His friends and acquaintances held Shaw in high esteem and long after his death remembered his warmth, wit, and charm. J. B. Pond, lyceum entrepreneur of Shaw's platform days, remembered him as "a delightful man to know personally—kind, gentle, sincere and very sympathetic, with an intense fondness for children."[20] High in praise of Shaw's character, as well as his literary subject matter, was his friend and comrade in platform humor, Charles H. Smith (Bill Arp): "He was a companionable man and talked without a strain. When he visited our little city of Rome our people gave him glad welcome, for he had been long ministering to their pleasure and in all his great and curious utterances he had never written a line that showed prejudice or malignity to our people or our section."[21] Shaw's friend and employer at the *New York Weekly,* Francis Shubael Smith, reminisced in his biography of Shaw: "In the first place he is the most amusing conversationist, and the most happy biped on earth. A half hour's conversation with 'Josh,' when he really feels good . . . is worth a day's travel to listen to. He has more quaint ideas, and original similes in his general talk, than any other man we wot of."[22]

Although like most writers Shaw enjoyed spells of being alone, he was essentially gregarious. Friendships he enjoyed and nurtured. Francis Smith observed that Shaw had "more friends, perhaps, than any other man in the city of New York" and spoke of how ubiquitous they were: "He generally walks to his residence uptown, a distance of about five miles, and if anybody is in a hurry, they better not accompany him, for they will have to stop about every five steps, till he converses a few minutes with a friend. How he can reach home at all, is a mystery to me."[23]

Among his acquaintances were many notable literary and artistic figures: Mark Twain, Charles Farrar Browne, James Whitcombe Riley, Charles H. Smith, Melville Landon (Eli Perkins), David Ross Locke (Petroleum V. Nasby), Benjamin Shillaber (Mrs. Partington), the cartoonist-illustrator Thomas Nast, William Cullen Bryant, and Bayard Taylor, to name the more renowned. Shaw met Browne while trying to publish his first book, and the two remained friends, as well as rival lecturers, for the remainder of their lives. Smith and Shaw met at Carleton's book store in New York—a rendezvous for authors—Smith having long anticipated meeting Shaw, who was his idol.[24]

Melville Landon, a long-time friend, years after Shaw's death remembered him as "a wonderful character!" and nostalgically recalled seeing "the old man now, with his long hair and tall, lank form leaning around on the book counters at Carleton's."[25] Shaw and Landon shared many an hour of witty verbal exchange. One such occasion in a cigar-smoke-filled hotel room in Saratoga in 1884, the year before Shaw's death, produced the following humorous interview which Landon loved to print:

"Mr. Billings, where were you educated?"
"Pordunk, Pennsylvania."
"How old are you?"
"I was born 150 years old—and have been growing young ever since."
"Are you married?"
"Once."
"How many children have you?"
"Doublets."
"What other vices have you?"
"None."
"Have you any virtues?"
"Several."
"What are they?"
"I left them up at Poughkeepsie."
"Do you gamble?"
"When I feel good."
"What is your profession?"
"Agriculture and alminaxing."
"How do you account for your deficient knowledge in spelling?"
"Bad spells during infancy, and poor memory."
"What things are you the most liable to forget?"
"Sermons and debts."
"What professions do you like best?"
"Auctioneering, base-ball and theology."
"Do you smoke?"
"Thank you, I'll take a Partaga first."
"What is your worst habit?"
"The coat I got last in Poughkeepsie."
"What are your favorite books?"
"My alminack and Commodore Vanderbilt's pocketbook."
"What is your favorite piece of sculpture?"
"The mile stone nearest home."
"What is your favorite animal?"
"The mule."

"Why?"

"Because he never blunders with his heels."

"What was the best thing said by our old friend Artemus Ward?"

"All the pretty girls in Utah marry *Young.*"

"Do you believe in the final salvation of all men?"

"I do—let me pick the men!"[26]

Landon's last visit with Shaw was on a streetcar in New York: "I think of him as I saw him then, sitting in the corner of the car, with his spectacles on his nose, and in a brown study. His mind was always on his work, and his work was to think out dry epigrams so full of truth and human nature that they set the whole world laughing."[27]

Twain, Nasby, Riley, and Shillaber were platform chums of Shaw's. Shaw and Riley were close friends and once appeared on the stage together.[28] Riley, among others, wrote a fitting poetic tribute to Shaw when he died. Billings, Nasby, and Twain comprised a triumvirate of sorts, for the three had frequently met at the Redpath Lyceum headquarters on School Street when they returned home after being on the circuit. The three enjoyed one another's company: they laughed and told stories together, attended lectures in a body, and even had a group portrait taken in 1873. In his autobiography, Twain describes at length a lecture which he, Billings, and Nasby had attended in Boston at which one De Cordova, a novice, had made a fool of himself before the discriminating Boston audience. Describing their group reaction to De Cordova's failure (the audience walked out on him), Twain wrote, "We drew a deep sigh; it ought to have been a sigh of pity for a defeated fellow craftesman, but it was not—for we were mean and selfish, like all the human race, and it was a sigh of satisfaction to see our unoffending brother fail."[29]

Shaw and Twain were good friends during the last fifteen years or so of Shaw's life. The two visited frequently when both were among Redpath's lecturers. Shaw was so enamored of his young friend that he made a special effort, while on a western lecture tour in the winter of 1873-74, to visit Twain's old office at the *Territorial Enterprise* and was impressed by seeing the desk on which Twain penned "The Celebrated Jumping Frog of Calaveras County."[30] Shaw frequently referred to Twain in his

lectures and writings. In *Everybody's Friend* (1874) he play-
fully published an apocryphal letter from Twain, one actually
written by himself. The letter shows the spirit of playfulness
that flourished between the two men. In it, Twain is respond-
ing negatively to an invitation from Shaw to contribute to the
New York Weekly; and, in so doing, Twain takes some characteristic jabs at Shaw's spelling techniques:

> I wish we could compromise; I wish it would answer for you
> to write one of these books, for me, while I write an almanac for you.
> But this will not do, because I cannot abide your spelling.
> It does seem to me that you spell worse every day.
> Sometimes your orthography makes me frantic.
> It is out of all reason that a man, seventy-five years of age, should
> spell as you do.
> Why do you not attend a night-school?
> You might at least get the hang of the easy words.
> I am sending you a primer by this mail which I know will help
> you, if you will study it hard.[31]

Shaw's loyalty to Twain is evident in a letter he wrote after
Twain had announced what Shaw considered a premature retirement from the platform. Shaw, who encouraged him to re-
consider, pointed out Twain's merits and attraction as a platform
speaker.[32] And Shaw's admiration and appreciation of his friend
are expressed in a biographical sketch he wrote of Twain in
1870. Among other comments, he wrote,

> Mark Twain iz about thirty years old last May, stands 6 foot 8
> and one quarter inches, iz the best deskriptive humorist living,
> smokes 40 cigars a day, skorns to part hiz hair in the middle, dont
> show enny dimond ring, haz got a monarchial mustash, loves woman
> as she iz, hates dogs, and eschews liquor. . . .
> He iz az genial (whare he loves) az gin and milk, but iz a charm-
> ing hater. . . .
> Report sez he wont lektur no more. I hope report lies (for once
> in its life) for Mark Twain, before an audience iz az easy tew
> understand az strawberries and cream.
> Hiz late book, called "Innocence Abroad," iz the most delishus
> history i ever perused. It haz all the integrity ov the multiplicashun
> table, and, at the same time, iz as full ov deviltry as Gullivers
> travels. . . .

He iz like all other genuine humorists, dont do the laffing himself, and really much prefers to say a good thing rather than a funny one. . . .

I beleave he iz not a church member, but mi impreshun is that hiz religion lies deep. . . .

I think now i could endorse Mark, (i dont mean hiz note, for i hav quit all kinds ov gambling,) he seems tew me to hav (with all the nervous excentricitys ov his natur) a spot for me. . . .

Mark Twain haz grate wit, he haz grate literary pretenshuns, but he iz a poor punster, and he ought tew be thankful for that, for thare aint nothing (unless it iz three cent gin) that iz more demoralizing than punning. . . .

Good bye, Mark Twain; let me advise you tew forgive the liberty i have taken in this sketch, and also let me ask yu (in behalf ov mi nabors) tew keep before the world with yure rare bits ov humor, for thare iz grate need ov sich az yu. . . .[33]

Loyalty was a trait that Shaw also extended to other friends. When friend Benjamin Shillaber was a struggling neophyte on the lecture platform in 1871, Shaw wrote him an encouraging letter, expressing his hope that Shillaber would find his next lecture season so successful that his "crib" would "burst with rye, oats and barley."[34] To Thomas Nast, friend and also main illustrator of Shaw's *Everybody's Friend*, he wrote this loyal message when Nast was publicly embarrassed by an interviewer who had printed erroneous information about Nast's household and family:

Dear Tommy:

I got your paper in which the "Interviewer" is handled. I will write some sentiments touching the "Interviewer" before long, when I get leisure, and you can illustrate it in your happy way, and between us we will scald the "kuss." Love to all.

Yours till deth,
Josh[35]

VII *Last Years*

Shaw spent his last years as a famous and successful author. When the *Hamilton Literary Monthly* commented on the college's distinguished alumnus and estimated his fortune at

$100,000, it could not have been wrong. Successful in almanacs, lectures, journalism, and books of essays and aphorisms, Shaw rivaled the popularity of any author of his day.

Unlike the bitter last years of his friend Twain, Shaw's old age was basically a comfortable, contented one. In 1877, he wrote an account, in the form of an open letter, of his life and present status in a tone that reflects his essential satisfaction with his life. He remarked

that i hav been suckcessfully marrid for over 30 years,—that i wear number 10 boots,—that i never studdid for the regular ministry,— that i dont possess enny hoss, and bugga,—that i way 190 pounds,— that i hav two dauters, and they are both united to men that sute me,—that i have no mother in law now extant,—that i dont keep enny dog.—that i beleaf in a futur state, and its proffits, and loss,—that i am not a free mason,—nor dont travel with torch lite proceshuns,— that i am very modest, but luv apple dumplins to deth,—that i am cluss on to 60 years old, and wuz once a farmer, and a dredphull poor one too,—that i never had the dispepshee, nor fidgets but once, and haint got rid ov them yet,—that i sprung from New England,— that i write for fun, and ducats combined,—that i am inklined to be honest,—that i dont di mi mustash,—that i am slo unto anger, and chuckfull ov hope.—that none ov mi ansesstors were hung, az fur bak az i hav sarched,—that i hav had sum lite tuches ov the rumatiz, and never run for offiss but what i got beat,—that i am temperanse to a fault, never drinking milk until it haz been thoroly skimmed,—that i haint got no pollytix, nor haff az mutch religion az i ought to hav,—that i hav been all mi life a looking for a ghost, and a honest man, and haint seen one yet,—that mi arly skooling waz not heavy.—These are sum ov the things i kno about miself. . . .[36]

Shaw's old age was an active one. Autumns, winters, and springs he lectured and wrote for the *Century* and the *New York Weekly;* but summers found him sojourning with his family at such scattered resorts as Saratoga, New York; Colorado Springs, Colorado; Hot Springs, Arkansas; Newport, Rhode Island; and the White Mountains of New Hampshire. For action, he preferred Saratoga: he was always a horse fancier, and there he could enjoy the races. For quietude and peaceful relaxation, he chose Colorado Springs or Hot Springs; there he could rest and think. He enjoyed solitude for himself and his wife more and more in his last years, for he apparently grew more withdrawn and somewhat taciturn toward the end.[37]

His health broke in the summer of 1884. He was ill most of the summer with an undetermined disease which took its toll on his vitality. The following year being difficult, Shaw and his wife—upon the advice of physicians—left for the Pacific coast in August 1885. Settling in Monterey, California, Shaw was temporarily reinvigorated by the Pacific air, and he and his wife enjoyed a stay there of almost two months. Shaw spent his time fishing and talking with admirers who had discovered his presence. He was even invited to lecture for a charity concern, but the lecture was never given. He died unexpectedly of apoplexy on the morning of October 14, 1885, while sitting on the porch of his hotel. His body was returned to his home town of Lanesboro where he was buried on October 24.

Perhaps national sentiment for the passing of Henry Wheeler Shaw is best summarized in the remark of Shaw's friend, J. B. Pond: "When 'Josh' passed away, I know that I lost a very dear friend, and that all who had known and heard him felt the same way. His was a noble spirit."[38]

"Affurisms"

UNDER such colorful titles as "Plum Pits," "Puddin & Milk," "Chips," "Koarse Shot," "Pepper Pods," "Hooks & Eyes," and "Jaw Bones," Shaw included groups of aphorisms in all his book-length works, as well as in the columns he wrote for the *Century Magazine* and the *New York Weekly*.[1] His major works —those containing the majority of his contributions in this line —are four: *Josh Billings, Hiz Sayings;*[2] *Josh Billings on Ice, and Other Things;*[3] *Everybody's Friend, or Josh Billings' Encyclopoedia and Proverbial Philosophy of Wit and Humor* (a compilation of almost everything he had published to that time);[4] and *The Complete Works of Josh Billings.*[5]

I A Compatible Mode

Because Shaw had the kind of mind that worked incisively and compactly, he felt most at ease in the literary form of the aphorism. Short sayings couching general truths were among the first of his literary productions (*Sayings* consisting of about half aphorisms), and they were the last pieces he contributed for publication in the "Uncle Esek's Wisdom" column for the *Century* and in his *New York Weekly* column.

Shaw's sayings are so natural that they give an air of ease and spontaneity of creation. Actually, however, they were often the result of hours of work on his part. Shaw's friend Melville Landon (Eli Perkins) wrote of finding Shaw composing aphorisms on a Madison Avenue streetcar:

That morning, when the old man espied me, he was so busy with his thoughts that he did not even say good morning. He simply raised one hand, looked over his glasses and said, quickly, as if he had made a great discovery:

"I've got it, Eli!"

"Got what?"

"Got a good one—lem me read it," and then he read from a crumpled envelope this epigram that he had just jotted down:

"When a man tries to make himself look beautiful, he steals—he steals a woman's patent right—how's that?"

"Splendid," I said. "How long have you been at work on it?"

"Three hours," he said, "to get it just right."

Landon adds, "Mr. Shaw always worked long and patiently over these little paragraphs. . . . When he got five or six written, he stuck them into his hat and went down and read them to G. W. Carleton . . . who was an excellent judge of wit, and he and Josh would laugh over them."[6]

Besides being compatible with Shaw, the aphorism appealed broadly to a reading populace bred in the American traditions of honesty, frugality, and general moral righteousness. Shaw knew this heritage, of course; and he remembered the influence that Poor Richard's sayings had asserted on an eighteenth-century audience, was aware of the attraction of sententious sayings in popular almanacs of the day, and appreciated the clever utterances of contemporary wits and phrase makers. The aphorism was both a comfortable and profitable mode to work in, and thus Shaw devoted serious attention to it. As Walter Blair has said, in discussing Shaw's dedication to pithy language, "He gave much time to his way of boiling down thoughts." No matter what the subject, "Josh Billings showed a great gift for squeezing much lore into a few words."[7] And Shaw did just that, faithfully practicing his belief that "ginowine proverbs ar like good kambrick needles—short, sharp, and shiny" (*Sayings*, 74).

II *Characteristics*

Aside from pithiness, there are several special characteristics of Shaw's aphorisms, and many of these traits are also applicable to his other writings. The most obvious is misspelling, a device Shaw employed in all his sayings except for those in the "Uncle Esek's Wisdom" column.[8] Although his method of spelling is basically phonetic, it lacks consistency. *Aphorism* is spelled *affurism* and *afferism* only a few pages apart, as are other pairs such as *fun, phun; hiz, his; tew, tu* (or 2); *by, bi; thare, there; true, tru;* and so forth. David Ross Locke (Petroleum V. Nasby) referred to this inconsistency in Shaw when being interviewed concerning his own method of misspelling:

Reporter.   Mr. Nasby, who is the worst speller, you or Mr. Billings?
Nasby.   Billings, by all odds. He does it on purpose. Mine is a scientific spelling, founded on phonetic principles, and, consequently, much in advance of the civilization of the age. It is constructed on a uniform principle.[9]

Actually, neither writer adhered to a "uniform principle."

The idea for using misspellings came directly to Shaw, as mentioned earlier, from Artemus Ward, whose essay on the mule won success because of it. But Ward was not the first to use the technique, for the influence that affected him and subsequently Shaw was initiated by the southern humorists of the 1840's and 1850's—particularly, as Jennette Tandy writes, by one Mozis Addums, the creation of Dr. George William Bagby of Richmond, Virginia. He was, observes Miss Tandy, "one of the first to discover the fact that unrestrained bad spelling is successful fun-making."[10] James Russell Lowell also used it, of course, in the *Biglow Papers*. It was a popular technique in a day when people were feeling just boastful enough of their new literacy, as Jesse Bier has stated,[11] "to laugh at the next lowest level from which most of the population were just barely lifting themselves."

In adopting this fad of the time, Shaw was not wholly pleased; for his first literary efforts had been written in correct spelling. And he personally considered cacography an unfortunate technique and one that in itself provides little humor. But, after first using it to gain success, he felt stuck with it, remarking, "When a man once puts on the cap and bells, no matter whether they bekum him or not, the world will insist upon hiz wearing them, however they pretend tew regret it" (*Friend*, 552). He also sensed, however, the psychological advantage of using misspellings and ungrammatical syntax. He knew that by dressing truth in these folksy, funny clothes it would be accepted. People, he believed, "will not take wisdom as wisdom."[12] He would see that they received it in appropriate dress.

Shaw's technique was received with acclaim, and he established fame not only as a wise, humorous philosopher but as a clever manipulator of language. Though later critics generally deplored his use of misspellings as a detraction from his wisdom (see Chapter 8), the majority of his contemporaries agreed with the opinion of Bill Arp that "his quaint-phonetic spelling spiced his maxims and proverbs, and made them attractive."[13]

Incorrect grammar and occasional distorted syntax for comic effect are other characteristics of Shaw's aphorisms. Pointing to specific forms, Henry Lewis Mencken made the interesting, if somewhat clinical, observation that Shaw "seems to have been the first humorist to employ *saw* for *seen*, as well as *did* for *done*, extensively."[14] It was common for Shaw to substitute the preterite for the past participle. Other examples of incorrect grammar are those usually found in dialectical humor, such as *hain't*, *ain't*, *hisself*, and *was* in place of *were* as the plural past tense of the verb *to be*. Actually, Shaw relied little on distorted syntax. He preferred clever wording and misspellings to loosely constructed sentences.

Other characteristics of the aphorisms lie outside the provinces of misspelling, slang, and malformed sentences. There are anticlimactic sentences ("Buty iz power; but the most treacherous one i kno ov" [*Works*, 251]), uses of understatement ("found the ice in a slippery condition" [*Ice*, 11]), and occasional puns and malapropisms. Shaw remarked that "a pun, tew be irresistable, don't ought to flavor ov malis aforethought; but wants tew cum sudden and apt, like a rat out ov his hole" (*Ice*, 123). Of too much punning he was wary, feeling that the pun is "a sort ov literary prostitushun in which futur happynesz iz swopped oph for the plezzure ov the moment" (*Ice*, 183-84).

Extraordinary or mixed figurative language—a trait which Walter Blair points out as characterizing all the literary comedians[15]—is also present in Shaw. His incongruous description of a pig, for example, reads: "His ears are like the lilac leaf, played upon bi the young zephurs at eventide, his silkaness is the woof ov buty, and his figger is the outline ov lovlaness" (*Sayings*, 75).

He characterizes love as making a man "fluent as a tin whissell, as limber as a boy's watch chain, and as perlite as a dansing master; his harte is as full ov sunshine as a hay field, and there aint any more guile in him than there is in a stik ov merlasses candy" (*Sayings*, 169). And, on the subject of laughter, Shaw prefers the laugh "that looks out ov a man's eyes fust, to see if the coast is clear, then steals down into the dimple ov his cheek, and rides in an eddy thare awhile, then waltzes a spell, at the korners ov his mouth, like a thing ov life, then busts its bonds ov buty, and fills the air for a moment with a shower ov silvery tongued sparks,—then steals bak, with a smile, to its lair, in the harte, tew watch again for its prey . . ." (*Sayings*, 229).

Shaw's way of sayings things is almost always original, whether he is making observations of his own such as "When a feller gits a goin down hil, it dus seem as tho evry thing had bin greased for the okashun" (*Sayings*, 83) and "I hav known folks whose *calibre* was very small, but whose *bore* was very big," (*Sayings*, 84) or rephrasing standard saws,[16] using the techniques of reversalism and antiproverbialism:

> Fust appearances are ced tu be everything. I dont put all mi fathe into this saying; i think oysters and klams, for instanze, will bear looking into. (*Sayings*, 17)
> "Truth iz stranger than ficshun"—that iz tew sum folks. (*Sayings*, 38)
> "Be sure yu are rite then go ahed"; but in kase ov doubt go ahed enny wa. (*Sayings*, 114)
> "Give me liberty, or giv me deth"—but ov the 2 I prefer the liberty. (*Ice*, 89)

Fresh, penetrating insights complement Shaw's originality of expression:

> There iz 2 things in this life for which we are never fully prepared, and that iz twins. (*Works*, 264)
> No man haz a rit tu be proud till he bekums entirely vartuous, and then he wont feel like being proud. (*Sayings*, 44)
> Preeching the gospel for nothin, is easy enuff, but preeching it fur 5 thousand a yere, and hav it sute, is anuther thing entirely. (*Sayings*, 77)

Humin natur is the same all over the world, cept in Nu England, and thar its kordin to sarcumstances. (*Sayings,* 82)

It alwus seemed to me that a left handed fiddler must pla the tune backwards. (*Sayings,* 85)

An ungrateful childe is the revenge of Heaven. (*Sayings,* 154)

The heart ov a true friend iz like a mirror; if yu look into it yu see yurself thare. (*Ice,* 216)

The top rounds ov a ladder are always the most dangerous. (*Ice,* 218)

I hav alwuss notissed that thare iz a grate deal ov good luk in industry, and a grate deal ov bad luk in lazyness. (*Friend,* 564)

It iz the little things in life that stir us up so mutch; thare iz 10 chances ov being stung bi a hornet whare thare aint one ov being stept on bi an elephant. (*Friend,* 571)

Virtew don't konsist in the absence ov the pashuns, but in the control ov them;—a man without enny pashuns iz simply as virtewous az a graven image. (*Works,* 214)

Occasionally, Shaw does not attempt to be humorous—just wise: "An insult tew one man iz an insult tew aul men" (*Sayings,* 37); "Passion makes more mistakes than ignorance duz" (*Ice,* 47); and "Buty iz a dangerous gift; for it is seldom accompanied with much virtue, energe, or wisdom," (*Ice,* 48).

In common with other humorists of his day, Shaw practiced various comic techniques that, as Blair says, created a humor "of phraseology rather than of character."[17] But in one major characteristic he differed considerably from the other humorists —in his imagery. Shaw had the rare poetical ability to convey his thoughts in sharp verbal pictures, surpassing the often trite, hyperbolic images of his contemporaries. Max Eastman, pioneer in recognizing Shaw's unusual way with imagery, labels Shaw a "poetic humorist," meaning that he is doing the same thing lightly that a poet does seriously: "using words in such a way as to give us visions, and even if he can, hallucinations."[18] Moreover, Eastman continues, visual imagery does not adequately characterize Shaw's writing because "poetry and poetic humor appeal to every sense."[19] An example is found in a comment Shaw made on courting: "Courting iz like 2 little springs ov soft water that steal out from under a rock at the fut ov a mountain and run down the hill side by side singing and dansing and spattering each uther, eddying and frothing and kaskading, now hiding under bank, now full ov sun and now full ov shadder, till bimeby tha jine and then tha go slow" (*Sayings*, 145).

And Eastman quotes three of Shaw's statements to prove his point that "not only sounds, smells, tastes and tactual sensations, but ideas, characters, emotions, *even actions when contemplated or described,* can form the material of poetry and poetic humor": "Cherries are good, but they are too mutch like sucking a marble with a handle tew it"; "Peaches are good, if you don't git enny ov the pin-feathers into yure lips"; "When boblinks sing their mouths git as full ov musik as a man's does of bones who eats fried herring for breakfast."[20]

Finally, Eastman dubs Shaw the "father of imagism," saying that Shaw was "the first man in English literature to set down on his page, quite like a French painter reared in the tradition of art for art's sake, a series of tiny, highly polished verbal pictures, and leave them there for what they might be worth."[21] Eastman even concludes that there is little in New England poetry up to Shaw's date "as graphic as some of this Poughkeepsie auctioneer's metaphors."[22]

These observations are highly apropos, for there is an originality in Shaw's language that transcends that of his close rivals —Ward, Nasby, and Phoenix. These others were more adept at creating dramatic and narrative situations; Shaw mastered the language and found success in penning terse, fresh expressions and vivid, highly effective images.

II *Subjects*

In the tradition of the Yankee crackerbox philosopher, who appeared to be knowledgeable on all subjects, Shaw had a thought and comment about almost everything. Though he did not discuss politics as much as Nasby nor enter into social satire as often as Ward and Phoenix, Shaw's sayings do run a remarkably broad gamut. Virtues, vices, love, literature, religion, marriage, business matters, and quirks of human nature appear as subjects of his aphorisms. Also included are philosophy, advice, and random views of certain universal subjects and problems.

Often, Shaw simply offers advice on various topics, revealing insights that are sage and pointed:

If yu are handsum, cultivate yure boots; if yu are hoamly, hoe yure branes. (*Ice,* 111)

Don't borry nor lend, but if you must do one, *lend.* (*Works,* 226)

Tew enjoy a good reputashun, giv publickly, and steal privately. (*Works,* 274)

"*Beware ov the dog!*" also ov the whispering man, and the loud-talking woman. (*Works,* 273)

Look out for thoze pholks who are familiar on short notiss, they are like hornets, they mean [to] *sting.* (*Works,* 314)

But Shaw was also interested in a number of specific topics. He was intensely concerned with writing and literature, and his interest is evident in numerous comments on the nature of good literature, principles of effective writing, the substance of poetry and satire, the qualities of great writers:

Poetri, tew be excellent, wants tew be like natur, but about 4 times az big. (*Ice,* 25)

I don't read enny boddy else's poetry but Homer's, upon the same principle that i alwus drink, when it is just as handy, out ov a spring, instead ov the outlet. (*Ice,* 104)

Originality in writing is as diffikult as gitting a fishpole by the side ov a trout brook—aul the good poles hav bin cut long ago. (*Ice,* 104)

About the most originality that enny writer kan hope tew arrive at honestly, now-a-days, is tew steal with good judgment. (*Ice,* 138)

Most ennyboddy can write poor sense, but there aint but few that can write good nonsense—and it alwus takes an eddycated man to appreciate it after it is writ. (*Ice,* 228)

Fine writing konsists in gitting the most thought into the shortest and simplest form. (*Friend,* 571)

Satire that iz seazonable and just iz often more effektual than law or gospil. (*Friend,* 591)

All the original thoughts have been uttered in the simplest words. When I read an abstruse sentence, I say, this writer has been stealing, and is trying to hide. (*Century,* XXVIII [September, 1884], 800)

Originality in writing has had its day. Nobody but a quack will strain for it. The best any one can do is to make the trail a little plainer for others to follow. (*Century,* XXIX [March, 1885], 798)

About the closely related subject of genius, Shaw observed:

Genius, like the yung eagle, don't hav tew make enny trial trips, but when it iz full fledged, pushes boldly out, even towards the sun. (*Works*, 266)

Genius iz like a hop vine, it will run, and spread enny how, and hav a whole lot ov haff wild hops on it, but tew be a good krop, it must be poled, and cut back, and suckered. (*Works*, 276)

Genius after all ain't ennything more than elegant kommon sense. (*Works*, 314)

One of Shaw's favorite pastimes was observing the human comedy with its multitudinous types and ruling passions. Among the most prevalent of human types, much to Shaw's chagrin, is the fool:

Thare are az menny old phools in this world as yung ones, and the old ones are the sillyest. (*Works*, 267)

A phool seems tew be a person who haz more will than judgment, and more vanity than either. (*Works*, 291)

I think the fools do more hurt in this world than the raskals. (*Sayings*, 67)

The fules in this wurld make about as much truble as the wicked du. (*Sayings*, 78)

God save the phools! and don't let them run out, for if it want for them, wise men couldn't get a livin. (*Sayings*, 92)

It iz dredful eazy tew be a phool—a man kan be one and not know it. (*Sayings*, 93)

Among the ruling passions, vanity predominates. Shaw often sounds like a cross between Swift and Franklin on the subject as he comments:

Thare iz sum disseazes that kant be kured even bi deth, for we oftin see them brake out on a man's tombstun more violent than ever. (*Sayings*, 178)

Success in life is very apt tew make us forget the time when we wasn't much. It iz jist so with the frog on the jump; he kant remember when he waz a tadpole—but other folks kan. (*Ice*, 204)

If a man wants tew git at hiz aktual dimenshuns, let him visit a grave-yard. (*Ice*, 204)

One ov the best temporary reliefs for vanity, that i kno ov, iz a sharp tutch ov the billyus kolick. (*Works*, 214)

The greatest blessing that the great and good God can bestow on enny human being iz humility. (*Works*, 219)

One ov the best temporary cures for pride and affektashun that i hav ever seen tried is sea sickness; a man who wants tew vomit never puts on airs. (*Works*, 247)

Love and marriage were two of his favorite subjects; and despite some disparaging remarks, Shaw usually treated them favorably (if cautiously):

Love haz a most vorashus appetight, but a poor digestion; what it feeds on most alwus distresses it. (*Works*, 240)

Love feeds on hopes and fears, and, like the chameleon, takes its color from what it feeds on. (*Works*, 267)

We speak ov "*falling in love*," without always thinking that it iz the only way tew git in love—we all stumble into it, and kan seldum tell *how* or *why*. (*Works*, 286)

Marrid life iz too often like a game ov checkers—the grate struggle iz tew git into the king row. (*Works*, 269)

A good wife iz a sweet smile from heaven. (*Works*, 273)

Marrying tew suit other folks iz the prudery ov politeness; i should as soon think ov begging pardon ov a thorn, for running against it. (*Works*, 274)

Marrying a woman for her munny is vera mutch like setting a rat-trap, and baiting it with yure own finger. (*Works*, 309)

There is an undeniable strain of skepticism and pessimism running through Shaw's humor—a trait that existed in a large portion of American humor during and immediately after the Civil War. In a period distorted by war, Reconstruction, and the emergence of the Gilded Age, with its rise of big business and social evils, the comedian's role was anything but a glib one. Struck by the serio-comic incongruities of the new American way of life, Shaw composed a type of humor that, as Jesse Bier has observed, included the ingredients of "sad comprehension, disillusion, pessimism, and cynical amorality."[23]

On the subject of man—the human condition and human progress—Shaw's sayings express this strain of skepticism. Sounding much like Twain, he comments:

Man was kreated a little lower than the angells and has bin gittin a little lower ever sinse. (*Sayings*, 83)

The studdy ov humin natur is a good deal like the studdy ov
dessekshun, yu finde out a good menny curis things, but it is a
nasty job after awl. (*Sayings,* 154-55)

Mi advise tu them who are about tu begin, in arnest, the journey
ov life, is tu take their harte in one hand and a club in the other.
(*Sayings,* 199)

If yu are happy, dont proklaim it tew the world, the world dont
luv tew hear about sich things. (*Sayings,* 215)

Necessity begot Invenshun, Invenshun begot Convenience, Convenience begot Pleasure, Pleasure begot Luxury, Luxury begot Riot
and Disease, Riot and Disease, between them, begot Poverty, and
Poverty begot Necessity again,—this is the revolushun ov man, and
is about aul he kan brag on. (*Ice,* 191)

"Man was kreated a little lower than the Angels,"—and it is lucky
for the said Angels that he was. (*Ice,* 192)

Thare are but phew things a man duz in this life, be they good,
bad, or indifferent, but what kan be traced to self-luv. (*Friend,* 589)

Human knowledge iz not very komprehensiv after all, for i hav
seen men who could kalkulate an eklips to a dot, who couldn't harness
a hoss tew save their lives. (*Works,* 249)

Vanity iz called a discreditabel pashun, but the good things that
men do kan oftner be traced tew their vanity than tew their virtew.
(*Works,* 257)

The same critical, skeptical attitude is found in the aphorisms
that treat such specific topics as politics, religion, women, and
the feminist cause. Showing both his amusement and pertur-
bation over politics and politicians, Shaw remarked, "Az a gineral
thing, if yu want tew git at the truth ov a perlitikal argyment,
hear both sides and beleave neither" (*Sayings,* 214). And "A
man running for offiss puts me in minde ov a dog that's lost—
he smells ov everybody he meets, and wags hisself all over"
(*Sayings,* 51). Religion attracted its share of Shaw's cynicism.
Shaw was not really antireligious; he was simply critical of
religious hypocrisy and man's misinterpretation and misman-
agement of religious principles. He found little of the genuine-
ness in religion that he felt necessary for a sound faith. He
opines:

Men will swear by their religion, will fight for it, will be martyrs
for it, will persecute others for it, will do anything and all things

for it, except observe it themselves. (*Century*, XXVIII [June, 1884], 318)

I wouldn't giv a shilling a pound for religion that yu kant take ennywhere out into the world with yu, even tew a hoss race, if yu hav a mind tew, without losing it. (*Works*, 264)

Religion iz nothing more than a chattel mortgage, excepted, and rekorded, az sekurity for a man's morality, and virtew. (*Works*, 290)

There are many people who have got a great deal more religion than common sense. Religion is excellent, but it isn't a substitute for common sense. (*Century*, XXVII [March, 1884], 798)

I hav got a fust rate opinyun ov resignashun, but i don't think enny man iz in dewty bound to thank the Lord every time sum careless cuss steps on hiz soar tow. (*Ice*, 35)

When various feminist groups such as the suffragettes rose to eminence in the last half of the nineteenth century, Shaw grew quite critical of woman and her role. He was definitely conservative on the matter of femininity. And he felt fully qualified—living with three women in his own family—to speak out on the qualities and shortcomings of the opposite sex. Of women in general he wrote:

Wimmin quite often possess superior tallents, but their genius lays in their pashuns. (*Works*, 241)

Woman haz no friendships. She either loves, despises, or hates. (*Works*, 247)

Wimmin are like flowers, a little dust ov squeezing makes them the more fragrant. (*Sayings*, 17)

I like a woman, (handsum if it iz convenient,) with more wisdom than larning, chaste, but not frozen, soft, but not silly, and fond, but not fussy, sich wimmin are skase, and are going tew be skaser. (*Sayings*, 175)

Of feminist crusades for rights and freedoms and of the effects of such missions, he was especially critical: "Tew git at the full sublimity ov a wimmins right lekturer, go tew her hum, and witness her old man striving to nuss their last baby, and notis what a dredful sloppy job he makes ov it" (*Ice*, 143-44); "Just about in proportion that a woman bekums famous away from home, she haz dun suthin she hadn't oughter" (*Ice*, 143). Even on the subject of wives, despite his own happy marriage, he could be slightly abusive: "If yu hav got a real good wife, kepe perfectly still, and thank God evry twenty minnitts for it" (*Sayings,* 51); "Their is one advantage in a plurality ov wifes; tha fite each other, insted ov their hustbands" (*Sayings,* 113); "I don't kno ov but one thing on arth that kan improve a good wife, and that iz buty" (*Sayings,* 39).

In spite of his occasional tone of skepticism and his penchant for criticism, Shaw's sayings, on the whole, affirm that life is worth living even if, as in a game of cards, "we must play what is dealt tew us, and the glory consists, not so mutch in winning, as in playing a poor hand well" (*Works,* 248). No Puritan either, Shaw felt that man must live vigorously and feel free to express his nature: "I don't belief in total abstinence, enny more than I belief in total blindness, but I do belief in the reasonable gratification ov awl the desires that God haz given us" (*Ice,* 49). A strong undercurrent running through the aphorisms implies that, although there are many faults in man, his institutions, and his actions, thoughts, and words, man must try to reap from life as abundant a harvest as possible. Shaw's view is that of the idealistic reformer and satirist: he loves at heart the subject he attacks, and he attacks it in order to make it better.

It is obvious, to conclude, that Shaw mastered the form of the aphorism and used it to comment on innumerable aspects of life. Crisp, pithy, witty, and original (in expression, if not always in source), his sayings pleased readers and lecture audiences alike. Perhaps the basis of their appeal is best summarized by Shaw's friend Bill Arp:

It is curious how we are attracted by the wise, pithy sayings of an unlettered man. It is the contrast between his mind and his culture. We like contrasts and we like metaphors and striking comparisons. The more they are according to nature and everyday life, the better they please the masses. The cultured scholar will try to impress us by saying "*facilis decensus averni,*" but Billings brings the same idea nearer home when he says, "when a man starts down hill, it looks like everything is greased for the occasion." We can almost see the fellow sliding down. It is an old thought that has been dressed up fine for centuries, and suddenly appears in everyday clothes.[24]

CHAPTER 3

Essays and Sketches

SINCE Shaw's initial fame as a man of letters was made as an essayist with his "Essa on the Muel," he devoted a substantial part of his talent to the essay and the sketch. Walter Blair, in fact, calls him "primarily an essayist" of the "Addison-Steele-Goldsmith tradition," for Shaw wrote "about all sorts of subjects in a fashion which was formal" (except in matters of spelling and grammar).[1] Shaw's essays and sketches are all brief; they rarely total more than five hundred words and many amount to a third of that. Although they generally pertain to a single main topic, they are somewhat loosely structured and often appear, on a cursory glance, to be little more than a series of related aphorisms. In that the single sentence bears so much burden, Shaw's essays resemble Emerson's in style. Constructed in this manner, they provide an air of ease and leisure in a familiar tone.

Shaw's method, as Joseph Jones has observed, is "an attractive medium; the total effect is pleasantly meditative, suggestive of thinking aloud, with just enough continuity to lend coherence and just enough looseness to allow unusual turns of phraseology to bob up in the most unexpected quarters."[2] The more extensively the essays are examined, the more evident is their true artistry. Most of them, upon close scrutiny, emerge as finely sculptured little pieces with definite unity and stylistic charm.

I *Soupe de Jour*

Unlike Nasby, Shaw usually refrained from centering his writings on the major economic, political, and social problems of his era. Essays such as the one on "Manifest Destiny"

(*Sayings,* 59-61) are rare exceptions in the Shaw canon, for most of his attention was devoted to lesser social concerns or to subjects of general human interest. In choosing subjects to satirize, for example, he was more inclined to single out the jargon of insurance-company questionnaires,[3] the folly of letter-answer columns in newspapers written by supposed authorities on all subjects from love to horses, the activities of a woman's liberation group, or the ridiculous aspect of a dandy man than he was to address himself to the growing evils of the Gilded Age.

This is not to say, however, that he ignored all current topics of interest. He had thoughts on many contemporary themes, as numerous essays reveal. On the subject of female education, for example, a moot topic of the day, he wrote several pieces expressing the view that, though women who desire formal learning should receive it, its effect on most women (and indirectly on their men) is questionable:

I haven't enny doubt, that you could eddicate wimmin so muchly, that tha wouldn't kno enny more about getting dinner, than sum ministers ov the gospil kno about preaching, and while tha mite translate one ov Virgils ecklogs tu a spot, tha couldn't translate a baby out ov a kradle, without letting it cum apart. . . . I believe in femail eddikashun, but i had ruther a woman cud beet me nussing a baby than tu feel that she cud beet me or enny other man in a stump speech or a lektur on veteranara praktiss. . . .

If Billings understands human natur, and he thinks he duz, thare aint nothing that a true woman luvs more than the hole ov a man's harte; and, in order tu git this, she haz got tu kno less than he duz, or maik him think so. I thank the lord that thare aint menny wimmin in the wurld who want tu know evry thing. I kalkerlate that 9 out ov evry 10 ov the wimmin who luv their huzbands and glory in their children, will sa that tha had ruther be looked down upon in luving tenderniss than to be looked up tu in silent aw.

He concludes: "i sa, elevate the wimmin, but if their heds and their hartes bekum antagonicks in the operashun, i shall continner tu think that luv, swapped for wizdom, iz a doutful gain to the wimmin and a pozatif loss to us poor mail-claid devils" (*Sayings,* 26-27).

Fashion was another subject that interested Shaw. One of his favorite pastimes at resort areas, which he loved to frequent, was observing people's dress and personal grooming. His opinion of the importance of fashion is unusual; for, instead of belittling it as a superficial human interest, he emphasizes its relevance to man's moral nature: it is "just az necessara tu govern men and wimmin with, az sivil law" (*Sayings*, 70). He feels the people who set fashions ought to be moral and virtuous because "the morals ov a people are just about az mutch in-flooensed by fashun az tha are by religun" (*Sayings*, 70). Ultimately, he sees fashion as containing definite merits: it "makes the poor ambishus, and it makes the rich affabil; it makes the vartuous cheerful, and it makes the humbly kind ov handsum, and thare iz no reson why it shud make the butiful wicked" (*Sayings*, 70).

Shaw leans just as favorably toward specific individual fashion vogues. He writes an essay on "Waterfalls," the rolls of hair worn low on women's necks, describing the effect on a nine-year-old girl, a nineteen-year-old, and a seventy-five-year-old woman. He concludes that he likes waterfalls and—punning—closes by saying, "It haz bin sed that they would run out, but this i think iz a error, for they don't show no leak yet. In the language of the expiring Canadian, on our northen frontier, I say—'Vive la Bag-a-tale'" (*Ice*, 108).

Of Shaw's contemporaries' reaction to music he is more critical, for he emphasizes the point that music basically appeals to the soul and not to the intellect. He observes that people, to be fashionable, pretend to understand such musical per-formances as opera on an intellectual level, declaring raptur-ously, "how bewitching! how delishus! how egstatick!" when "nineteen out ov evry twenty-one ov them wouldn't kno it if the performance was a burlesk on their grandmother" (*Sayings*, 118). Shaw takes the typical crackerbox philosopher's view of musical performances, sharing the anticultural outlook of his friend John Phoenix, who spoofed the symphonic performance in his "Musical Review Extraordinary."[4]

In an essay ridiculing another minor interest of the day, spiritualism, Shaw reports of sitting in on a séance and ob-serving one Augustus Bloodgood contacting the ghost of a Miss

Jerusha Perkins. In a spoof of conversations between persons on either side of the mortality barrier, Shaw has Miss Perkins discuss shopping in heaven ("Dri goods is cheap here"), the weather there (it "iz fine, and there iz evry prospeck ov krops ..."), and other rather pedestrian topics for a spirit to be concerned with (*Sayings*, 128-30). In short, the picture is just like one of earth; and Shaw makes his point about the meaninglessnesss of the séance fad.

Shaw the moralist is never very distant in his essays. In an essay by the same title as one of his lectures, "The Devil's Putty and Varnish" (*Sayings*, 56-58), he criticizes the trend of smoothing over scandalous and injurious deeds and practices. An unnecessary duel resulting in an "elegant murder" is called "an affair ov honnor"; if a man embezzles, the act is referred to by the examining committee as "a diskrepansy in hiz akounts"; when two young drunken, horse-and-buggy drivers are killed because of their ineptitude, the affair is reported as a "Fatal acksident"; and, when two trains collide because of the recklessness of the drunken crew, the wreck is dubbed "an unavoidable katastrophe." Shaw concludes by warning, "The Devil furnishes putty and varnish, free ov expense, tew hide the frauds and guilt ov men" (58).

Thus from female education to problems of slack morality, Shaw was concerned with the subjects of the day and devoted many of his essays to them. A major aspect of his popularity and effectiveness with his audience lay in his being able to comment on particular instances as well as universal conditions. When his readers wanted to know what "Josh" had to say on a matter, they were never left wondering long.

II *The Antic Muse*

However serious a moralist and philosopher Shaw was, he was at the same time a highly successful literary funny man. One reason for his success in the realm of humor is that he thought extensively about the nature and roles of wit and humor and about the value and effects of laughter. He and Bret Harte have even been called "our first tentative comic theoreticians."[5] In several essays devoted specifically to humor, as well as in random passages in other essays, Shaw expressed his incisive views about the comic art.

In one of his several excellent essays on laughter (*Ice*, 83-84), Shaw points out that laughter is the special property of man (since the other animals cannot laugh) and is a vital sign of life, beneficial alike to mind and body. The power to laugh "is the power to be happy." The laugh is "an index ov karackter." Laughter accomplishes many things and has numerous virtues:

Laffing keeps oph sickness, and haz conquered az menny diseases az ever pills have, and at mutch less expense.—It makes flesh, and keeps it in its place.—It drives away weariness and brings a dream ov sweetness tew the sleeper.—It never iz covetous.—It ackompanys charity, and iz the handmaid ov honesty.—It disarms revenge, humbles pride, and iz the talisman ov kontentment.—Sum have kalled it a weakness—a substitute for thought, but really it strengthens wit, and adorns wisdom, invigorates the mind, gives language ease, and expreshun elegance.—It holds the mirror up tew beauty; it strengthens modesty, and makes virtue heavenly. It iz the light ov life; without it we should be but animated ghosts. It challenges fear, hides sorrow, weakens despair, and carries haff ov poverty's bundles.—It costs nothing, comes at the call, and leaves a brite spot behind.—It iz the only index ov gladness, and the only buty that time kannot effase.— It never grows old; it reaches from the cradle tew the grave. Without it, love would be no pashun, and fruition would show no joy.—It iz the fust and the last sunshine that visits the heart; it was the warm welkum ov Eden's lovers, and was the only capital that sin left them tew begin bizzness with outside the Garden ov Pardise.

In another piece on laughter (*Sayings*, 228-29), Shaw catalogues and discusses types of laughs. There are laughs that "dont make enny noise" and others that "dont make ennything but noise"; some people have music in their laughter, and some "laff just az a rat duz, who haz caught a steel trap, with his tale." Some laughs "cum rompin out ov a man's mouth," while others "are az kold and meaningless az a yesterday's buckwheat pancake." Shaw dislikes a giggle: it "iz like the dandylion, a feeble yeller, and not a bit ov good smell about it," but he believes any kind of laugh is better than none. The important thing is that man make use of his special ability and laugh for health and for a sense of well-being.

Switching attention from laughter to its cause, humor, Shaw
tries to arrive at a satisfactory definition of wit and humor.
Though he feels his effort is ultimately unsuccessful, he makes
some meaningful distinctions. Wit, he feels, "may be the bringing together two ideas, apparently unlike, and hav them prove
tew be a cluss match." He explains and exemplifies: "I don't
serpose that there would be enny grate quantity ov wit in yure
telling sumboddy that yure gal was as hansum as a rose, but
thare might possibly be sum wit into it if yu should go on and
say that she was as frail, and as thorny, too" (*Ice*, 229). He
notes that there are various kinds of wit, one of which is punning; but he thinks little of the pun, feeling that it is an attempt
to make words pass for ideas. Though there is undoubtedly
some measure of wit in the pun, "it is something like sticking
a pin into a man, just for fun, and then ask him tew join in the
joke" (*Ice*, 230).

Humor, as opposed to wit, is gentler. Shaw compares it to heat
lightning: it is "not the original artikle that gashes the heavens
with a flaming sword and makes a fellow's hair get up on end and
ake with astonishment. Humor don't dazzle, don't knock a man
down with a sparkle; it is more a soothing syrup, sumthing tew
tickle, without enny danger ov throwing the patient into fits"
(*Ice*, 229-30). Ultimately feeling his definitions of each subject
inadequate, Shaw compares wit and humor with the intangible
pleasure in kissing: "Thare is a peculiar kind ov bewitchment
in awl three ov them, that evryboddy can acknowledge better
than they can pictur out" (*Ice*, 230).

American versus British humor is the subject of Shaw's essay
"Amerikans." He believes that Americans like stronger, more
caustic humor and that they leave the subtler form to the
English:

Amerikans love caustick things; they would prefer turpentine
tew colone-water, if they had tew drink either.

So with their relish of humor; they must hav it on the half-shell
with cayenne.

An Englishman wants hiz fun smothered deep in mint sauce, and
he iz willin tew wait till next day before he tastes it.

If you tickle or convince an Amerikan yu hav got tew do it quick.

An Amerikan luvs tew laff, but he don't luv tew make a bizzness ov it; he works, eats, and haw-haws on a canter.

I guess the English hav more wit, and the Amerikans more humor. We havn't had time, yet, tew bile down our humor and git the wit out ov it. (*Ice*, 183)

Finally, American humor is more sensational than its British counterpart: "Sumthing new, sumthing startling iz necessary for us az a people" (*Ice*, 184). The English might scoff at Americans for this trait, but it is essential to their nature, Shaw feels.

In the same essay Shaw also discusses the difficulty of writing effective humor and points out that many people attempt it and fail: "Evryboddy that writes expeckts tew be wize or witty—so duz evrybody expect tew be saved when they die; but thare iz good reason tew beleave that the goats hereafter will be in the majority, just az the sheep are here." And he admonishes, "Don't forget *one* thing, you hav got tew be wize before yu kan be witty; and don't forget two things, a single paragraff haz made sum men immortal, while a volume haz been wuss than a pile-driver tew others . . ." (*Ice*, 184).

III *Sense and Sensibility*

Undergirding Shaw's essays is a basic keen sensitivity, a perception of life's most meaningful values, and a sense of devotion to and love of life. Enhancing this sensitivity is a style often remindful, as Max Eastman indicated, of the poet. In his best pieces Shaw handled his prose with a delicacy, concision, and balance that lend a definite poetic effect. Such a work is his essay entitled "Hartes"—a fitting analysis of a child's heart:

SUM hartes is trumps.

The little child's harte has a host ov shaddery things in it, fairy ghostesses, in the distanse, without mutch form,—in the fore-ground, tops, and marbles, rag dolls, and sweet whissels; christmas, with the little old esquire in his tights, and frisky span, loaded with wares for a baby market; dreams without enny meaning, little jelosys, little hopes and curious fears,—strange invoice, but life's capital, in which sleep giants and pigmys, happiness and misery.

Life's capital! which can't be increased, but which may aul be lost.

The little child's harte! look down into it, it is like the vault ov
a wild-flower; apparently tenantless but full ov little sekrets, sekrets—
unknown tew itself,—sekrets worth knowing,—life's capital.

Sweet little vault whare God has locked up creation's destiny.
(*Ice,* 127)

The vignette obviously has a grace and charm of style and diction along with poetic balance and concision. It is a sensitive,
artistic account of a child's nature.

Shaw's insight into human phenomena is never keener than in
his piece on the firstborn baby in a family. The excitement of
one of life's most significant experiences exudes from almost
every line of the essay:

The fust baby has bekum one ov the fixed stars ov life; and ever
since the fust one was born, on the rong side of the gardin ov Eden,
down tew the little stranger ov yesterday, they hav never failed
tew be a budget ov mutch joy—an event ov mutch gladness. Tew
wake up some cheerful morning, and cee a pair ov soft eyes looking
into yours—to wonder how so much buty could have been entrusted
to you—to sarch out the father, or the mother, in the sweet little
fase, and then loze the survey, in an instant of buty, as a laffing
Angel lays before you—tew pla with the golden hare, and sow fond
kisses upon this little bird in yure nest—tiz this that makes the fust
baby, the joy ov awl joys—a feast ov the harte. Tew find the pale
Mother again bi yure side, more luvly than when she was wooed—
tew see a new tenderness in her eye, and tew hear the chastened
sweetness ov her laff, as she tells something new about "Willie"—tew
luv her far more than ever, and tew find oftimes a prayer on yure
lips—tiz this that makes the fust baby a fountain ov sparkling
plezzure. Tew watch the bud on yure rosebush, tew ketch the fust
notes ov yure song-bird, tew hear the warm praze ov kind frends,
and tew giv up yure hours tew the trezzure—tiz this that makes
the fust baby a gift that Angels hav brought yu. Tew look upon
the trak that life takes—tew see the sunshine and shower—tew plead
for the best, and shrink from the wust—tew shudder when sikness
steals on, and tew be chastened when death comes—tiz this—oh!
tiz this that makes the fust baby a hope upon arth, and a gem up
in heaven. (*Sayings,* 226-27)

Shaw's respect for the natural customs and routines of life is
always present in his works. His essay on "Courting" epitomizes
his attitude and tone:

Courting is a luxury, it is sallad, it is ise water, it is a beveridge, it is the pla spell ov the soul. The man who has never courted haz lived in vain; he haz bin a blind man amung landskapes and waterskapes; he has bin a deff man in the land ov hand orgins, and by the side ov murmuring canals. Courting iz like 2 little springs ov soft water that steal out from under a rock at the fut ov a mountain and run down the hill side by side singing and dansing and spattering each uther, eddying and frothing and kaskading, now hiding under bank, now full ov sun and now full ov shadder, till bimeby tha jine and then tha go slow. I am in favor ov long courting; it gives the parties a chance to find out each uther's trump kards, it iz good exercise, and is jist as innersent as 2 merino lambs. Courting iz like strawberries and cream, wants tew be did slow, then yu git the flaver. (*Sayings,* 145)

Shaw occasionally even wrote in a transcendental mood.[6] The essay-sketch "My Fust Gong" recalls the setting in which he supposedly heard the gong of a bell for the first time. He was sitting on a tavern step, smoking and watching the sun set and lazy boats meandering through the Erie Canal. The effect was hypnotic: 'Mi entire sole was, as it ware in a swet, i wanted tu climb, i felt grate, i aktually grew. Thar ar things in this life tu big tu be trifled with, thar ar times when a man brakes luce from hisself, when he sees speerits, when he kan almost tuch the moon, and feels as tho he kud fill both hands with the stars ov heavin and almost sware he was a bank president. Thats what ailed me" (*Sayings,* 176).

It is in writings such as these that Shaw's artistic superiority to the average literary comedian and witty philosopher becomes evident. Even the other major comedians—Artemus Ward, Petroleum V. Nasby, and John Phoenix—wrote nothing that shows the measure of sensitivity and perception of human values that Shaw demonstrates. Of his circle, only Mark Twain's work is similar in depth of feeling and insight.

IV *The Proper Subject of Mankind*

Man was a fascinating subject to Shaw. Any being that once had a home as beautiful and satisfactory as Eden and then lost it has to be a most intriguing, if puzzling, subject. In "A Short and Very Affekting Essa on Man," Shaw alludes to that fact and dubs man "a moste magnificant failure" (*Sayings*, 99), a phrase reminiscent of some of Twain's comments. "Failure" man might be, but he is still to Shaw the most significant being alive and deserving of full-time study. Shaw, with his acute observer's eye, was particularly prone to classify man into various types or categories, classifications that run an exhaustive gamut. Shaw types man according to such conditions as his disposition, social and economic status, personal appearance, marital status, physical characteristics, occupations, religious and political beliefs, and moral (or immoral) inclinations.

Shaw's human museum is composed of the Fault-Finder, whom Shaw avoids like he does the smallpox ("bekause i am a looking after bright things and haint got enny to lose" [*Sayings*, 153]); "Live Yankees," who "are chuck full of karakter and sissing hot with enterprize and curiosity" and who love liberty "with a red pepper enthuziasm" and believe New England "kan whip the universe" (*Ice*, 20-21); "the Shyster" and "the Shinner" (*Friend*, 569-70), the former a cheap lawyer despised by everyone, the latter a man who is always on the run trying to accomplish something but rarely having anything to show for his efforts; and "Natral and Unnatral Aristokrats," the latter only pretending to aristocratic station on grounds of pedigree and money, while the former qualifies on the basis of virtue: "When the world stands in need ov an aristokrat, natur pitches one into it, and furnishes him papers without enny flaw in them" (*Friend*, 581).

Shaw classifies widows as "The Lone," "The Grass," and "The Star Spangled Banner Widder" (*Sayings*, 140-42). "The Lone" is the good, gray old lady who, remaining devoted to the memory of her husband, has reached a compromise in life between grief and satisfaction with her state. "The Grass" widow is a racy young divorcée who has separated from her husband on grounds of "unkongenial tempraments." She has a licentious nature, a roving eye, reads *Don Juan*, and "hides Boccaccio's tales under her pillow." The "Star Spangled" is the spoiled darling who married a man because his name was "Alphonzo," and she mourns for him "in at least 50 feet ov krape." She has all the finery imaginable, has been educated in all the languages (except English), but "has more chastity than sens, and more Vartue than affekshun."

Shaw wrote innumerable monographs of one page or less on almost every kind of human being imaginable, singling out their ruling passions or chief characteristics. Representative titles of these sketches are "The Pompous Man," "The One Idea Man," "The Happy Man," "The Henpecked Man," "The Cunning Man," "The Loafer," "The Positiff Man," "The Cross Man," "The Pashunt Man," "The Funny Man," "The Honest Man," "The Limber Man," "The Square Man," "The Oblong Man," "The Perpendiklar Man," "The Precise Man," "The Effeminate Man," "The Jealous Man," "The Annonymous Man," "The Stiff Man," "The Model Man," and "The Neat Person" (*Works*, 326-59). As Shaw develops his portrait of each type, his thorough knowledge of mankind is salient. Since each person comes alive in the brief space devoted to him, this quality prevents the portrait from being a mere stereotype. These monographs are heightened by that spark of wit and originality so germane to all of Shaw's writings.

V *The Animal Fair*

"I take a deep interest in moste awl the animils . . . ," wrote Shaw in 1865 (*Sayings*, 160), a statement which introduces one of the most significant subjects of his essays. For next to man, he was fascinated with the variety of species and characteristics of the animal world. Walter Blair has referred to this captivation as perhaps Shaw's "greatest individual quirk."[7]

Shaw's method in the animal essays is to single out the peculiar characteristics of each animal, indicate whether these traits are favorably or unfavorably disposed toward men, state his findings humorously, and occasionally attach a fitting moral to the discourse. Though Shaw shares with Aesop the tendency to draw moral parallels with the human world, he differs from his classical precursor in that he concentrates more on natural history than on moralistic parables involving animal characters and actions. His approach also varies from that of another American humorist who dealt with the animal world—the Old Southwest humorist Thomas Bangs Thorpe—whose observations on animals focused on the animal as potential game for man. Shaw was uninterested in animals as game (with the exception of fish); moreover, his menagerie is usually composed of non-game animals, domesticated species, and even insects.

His most famous essay belongs to the animal group—the piece on the mule that made him widely known when he was struggling for literary recognition in the early 1860's. A good representation of Shaw's writing on animals, it contains the humorous delineation of the mule's nature (the humor involving gross exaggerations, anticlimactic sentences, and malapropisms), the author's subjective opinion of the animal's strengths and weaknesses (mainly the latter in this case), and a reference to the mule's likeness to man ("very korrupt at heart"). This essay certainly merits quoting in its entirety:

The mule is haf hoss, and haf Jackass, and then kums tu a full stop, natur diskovering her mistake. Tha weigh more, akordin tu their heft, than enny other kreetur, except a crowbar. Tha kant hear enny quicker, nor further than the hoss, yet their ears are big enuff for snowshoes. You kan trust them with enny one whose life aint worth enny more than the mules. The only wa tu keep them into a paster, is tu turn them into a medder jineing, and let them jump out. Tha are reddy for use, just as soon as they will du tu abuse. Tha haint got enny friends, and will live on huckel berry brush, with an ockasional chanse at Kanada thissels. Tha are a modern invenshun, i dont think the Bible deludes tu them at tall. Tha sel for more money than enny other domestik animile. Yu kant tell their age by looking into their mouth, enny more than you kould a Mexican cannons. Tha never hav no disseease that a good club wont heal. If tha ever die tha must kum rite tu life agin, for i never herd nobody sa "ded mule." Tha are like sum men, very korrupt at harte; ive known them tu be good mules for 6 months, just to git a good chanse to kick sumbody. I never owned one, nor never mean to, unless there is a United Staits law passed, requiring it. The only reason why tha are pashunt, is bekause tha are ashamed of themselfs. I have seen eddikated mules in a sirkus. Tha kould kick, and bite, tremenjis. I would not sa what I am forced tu sa again the mule, if his birth want an outrage, and man want tu blame for it. Enny man who is willing tu drive a mule, ought to be exempt by law from running for the legislatur. Tha are the strongest creeturs on earth, and heaviest, ackording tu their sise; I herd tell ov one who fell oph from the tow path, on the Eri kanawl, and sunk as soon as he touched bottom, but he kept rite on towing the boat tu the nex stashun, breathing thru his ears, which stuck out ov the water about 2 feet 6 inches; i did'nt see this did, but an auctioneer told me ov it, and i never knew an auctioneer tu lie unless it was absolutely convenient. (*Sayings,* 13-14)

Occasionally Shaw introduced an animal essay by making some comment on nature or the animal kingdom in general, a technique that reveals his over-all philosophy of nature. In the essay "Sum Natural History" (*Ice*, 14-19), for example, his introduction concerns natural history itself:

THARE iz no tuition so cheap and so handy az natral history.

It prevails evrywhere; the cockroach and the behomath are built out ov it, the lizard and the elephant are full ov it, it is the monkey's right bower, and the kangaroo's best jump.

The grass, the dandelion and the spinnage are its children; it is the language ov creeping things, the majesta ov the mountin, the soul ov the talking brook, and the inspiration ov the lambkin's tail.

Natral history iz dogg cheap.

To open our eyes, and think while we are looking iz aul the capital necessary for the naturalizing bizzness.

Who wouldn't be a naturalizer, when natur makes such cheap sacrifices upon aul her alters, and holds the insense under our very nozes?

He then discusses three unpleasant inhabitants of the natural world: grasshoppers, who "don't seem tew be acktually necessary for our happiness, but they may be; we don't even know what we want most"; bedbugs, who if created for some wise purpose "must hav took the wrong road, for there kant be enny wisdom in chawing a man aul night long, and raising a family, besides, tew foller the same track"; and fleas: "It is impossible to do ennything well with a flea on you, except sware, and fleas aint afraid ov that; the only way iz tew quit bizzness ov awl kinds and hunt for the flea, and when you have found him, he ain't thare. Thiz is one ov the flea mysterys, the fackulty they hav ov being entirely lost jist as soon as you hav found them."

An excellent example of Shaw's using animal characteristics as a means of delineating human types is his essay on whisperers and gossips. Entitled "The Buzzers," the piece compares such people to bumblebees and does so in a way (mainly through careful choice of diction) to lower man to the level of insects:

OV AWL the insekts or even animals, who occupy two legs and breathe the same kind ov air, and drink the same kind ov water that other folks do, thare is not a more distressingly bizzy and uncomfortably obnoxious one, than yure whisperer.

I mean now those men or those wimmin whose position in the world gives them the title tew be listened to, and even beleaved, who spend their lives like a bumbel bee on the wing, from flower to flower, and from thistle to thistle, buzzing and whispering.

These kind ov bumbel beeze deal only in sekrets ov the most delikate or dreadful kind, which they entrust to you with awl the importance and aimable reserve that distinguishes the intimate frend.

There is nothing in the world that would give them more pain or confusion (if you can beleave them) than to have their buzzes repeated, and yet, in truth, nothing would giv them more mortifikation if they were not. . . .

I know not from what ambishun this buzzing springs, unless it is the vanity ov knowledge, or the skarcity ov news; but one thing is certain, that no more inveterate workers kan be found—they are emphatikally the early birds who find the worm; they are the bizzy bees ov thrift, and they are your provident pissmires who alwus have corn in their cells against the calamity ov a wet day. . . . These insekts know evry marriage that is on the ways, and just when it is tew be launched; they know awl the slips and the slipshods within a circle of twenty leagues or more; they guess at outrages and divine bankrupcys; they hear ov elopements in the breath ov the morning, and see the spektral shaddow ov a domestik brawl stealing on tiptoze amid the gray ov the evening; they know the crimes ov evrybodys grandfather, and remember, just like a book, the time when the wife ov esquire Baker was no better than she should be. . . .

I hav searched the musty annals ov primogeniture, and hav dove down deep into the labarynths of succession, to trace the literal descent ov these slander-breeding and birth-giving scorpions, and found that about four thousand years ago, *Envy* begot *Malice,* *Malice* begot *Revenge,* and *Revenge* had twins—one was a common thief and the other was a buzzer.

Nature seems, in the production of Buzzers, to hav transgressed one ov her most aimable laws: I mean, the grate parsimony she generally shows in inflikting humanity with venemous reptiles. . . .

If these pests ov humanity were not wuss in their malice than a pizen snake without rattles, or meaner in their mischief than the robber ov birds nests, I would try and hunt up an apology for them, or at least, would attribute to an eager curiosity, or the vanity ov being thought a kind ov sub-treasury ov other folks' confidence, what is quite too often too gross to be set down only in the calender ov crimes.

Good-bye buzzers, ov high and low degree—yu that buzz in petticoats, and yu that buzz in britches; I hav but one opinion ov you, and that is—a dreadful mean one. (*Ice*, 219-22)

That scarcely a common animal or insect eludes Shaw's pen is evident from a list of selected essay titles taken from the *Complete Works.* From the insect world he discusses "Angle Worms," "The Pissmire," "Aunt and Grasshopper," "Snails," "The Fly," "The Bumble Bee," "The Cursid Musketo," "The Hornet," "The Cockroch," "Bed Bugs," "The Aunt," "The Grub," "The Lady Bug," and the "Devils Darning Needle."

In the wild animal kingdom Shaw seems chiefly interested in birds and snakes, as he writes on "The Crow," "The Robbing," "The Swallo," "The Hawk," "The Partridge," "The Hosstritch," "The Parrot," "The Bobalink," "The Eagle," "Sandy Hill Crane," "The Blujay," "The Quail," "The Woodkok," "The Guina Hen," "The Goslin," "The Snipe," and then "Striped Snake," "The Adder," "The Blue Racer," "The Blak Snaik," "The Milk Snaik," "The Rattlesnaix," "The Hoop Snaix," "The Anakondy," "The Garter Snaix," "The Eel Snaix," "The Sarpent Snaix," and the "Kopper-hed Snaix."

But he also singles out other wild animals for attention: "The Monkey," "The Pole Kat," "The Weazel," "The Mouse," "The Fox," "The Possum," "The Rabbit," "Raccoon and Pettyfogger," "The Tree Tud," "The Porkupine," "The Bat," and "The Meddo Mole." And he treats such sea and water "animals" as "The Clam," "The Crab," "The Codfish," "The Mackrel," "The Polly-wogg," "The Bullhead," and "Mud Turkles."

On the domestic animal front he selects for discussion "Nu Foundland and Tarrier," "The Rat Tarrier," "The Yaller Dog," "Cat and Kangaroo," "The Poodle," and "Kats." And from the farm he chooses "Roosters," "A Hen," "The Gote," "Goose Talk," "Essa on Swine," "The Duk," "The Turkey," and "Not enny Shanghi."

Finally there are some miscellaneous and even fictitious animals and insects such as "The Game Chicken," "The Hum Bugg," and "The Bugg Bear" (all the above from *Works*, 97-205).

Shaw's interest in the animal kingdom, in short, was as inexhaustible as the phyla and species themselves. Only such a curious interest, combined with droll humor and insight, could produce the following thoughts on the snake, the cat, and the dog:

I divide snaiks into one class, to wit, the devilish:
They are ov much antiquity, having appeared about the same time that Adam did. The exact purpis for which tha was built hain't been explored yet; but one thing is sartin, tha are quite slippery and eazy to bend. Tha travel on thair bellys, and go down hill the moste eazyest; this is owing tew the fack that tha hain't got enny good rigging tew hold back with.... (*Sayings,* 157)

I hav studdyed cats clussly for years, and hav found them adikted tew a wild state. Tha haint got affekshun, nor vartues ov enny kind, tha will skratch their best friends, and wont ketch mice unless tha are hungry. It haz bin sed that tha are good tu make up into sassages; but this iz a grate mistake, i hav bin told bi a sassage maker that tha dont kompare with dogs. Thare is one thing sartin, tha are verry anxious tew liv, yu ma turn one inside out, and hang him up bi the tale, and az soon az yu are out ov sight, he will manage tew turn back summerset and cum around awl rite in a fu days. It iz verry hard wurk to looze a cat. If one gits carried oph in a bag bi mistake a grate ways into the kuntry, tha wont sta lost onla a short time, but soon appear tew make the family happy with their presence.... (*Sayings,* 40)

Dogs are various in kind, and thanks tew an allwise Providence, tha are various in number. Tha are the onla animil ov the brute perswashun, who hav voluntary left a wilde stait ov natur, and cum in under the flag ov man. Tha are not vagabones bi choise, and luv tew belong to sumbody. This fac endears them tew us, and i have alwas rated the dog az about the seventh cusin tew the humain specious. Tha kant talk, but tha kan lick yure hand, this shows that their hearts iz in the plase where uther folks' tungs iz. Dogs in the lump are useful, but tha are not alwas priffittable in the lump.... It is dredful hard work for me to sa a hard word agin a dog; the wag ov their tails is what takes me. Enny man who will abuze a dog, needn't ask me to luv him, or pra for him. Enny man who will abuze a dog will abuse a woman, and enny man who will abuse a woman is thirty-five or forty miles miles [*sic*] meaner than—a pale paller dog. (*Sayings,* 64-66)

As an essayist, then, Shaw was familiar, succinct, humorous, and diverse. Without indulging in major reform diatribes, he was very much interested in contemporary topics and in human improvement. His interest in both the human and animal realms was inexhaustible, and he enjoyed exploring the multitudinous types in both realms. Predominant in his essays is the strain of optimism and good humor that overshadows the occasional notes of criticism. Considering the range and nature of his utterances, Bill Arp's appraisal of Shaw as being "Aesop and Ben Franklin, condensed and abridged"[8] is most apropos.

VI *Sketches*

Shaw's essays on human and animal types border on the form of the sketch, mainly because of their descriptive material; but they are undoubtedly primarily essays in method, scope, and effect. A number of other pieces, however, are true sketches which dwell descriptively on a single subject. Shaw was particularly fond of writing sketches of his favorite vacation haunts; therefore, a number of pieces are devoted to Long Branch,[9] the seaside resort town in New Jersey. Sojourning there frequently during summers to restore his "buty and health," Shaw wrote accounts of his experiences, filling them with observations of the events and customs of that place: surf swimming, drinking (strong Jersey whiskey and apple toddy), horse racing, "politicking," gambling, crab eating, flirting and courting, and watching for the "Big Snake," a legendary serpent which supposedly appeared periodically at Long Branch beach. He describes the hotels, the bars, the beachhouses, and the swimmers (expressing surprise over males and females entering the water hand in hand and swimming together). Shaw liked the pace and variety of life at Long Branch, was thrilled by the ocean, and always reluctantly returned home at the end of the season, perhaps having lost "50 pounds in munny, and gained 10 pounds in meat" (*Sayings*, 133).

Saratoga Springs, New York, a famous tourist retreat and spa, is the subject of five sketches.[10] Shaw enjoyed vacationing there almost as much as he appreciated Long Branch. Thrilled with the excitement and bustle of the area, he wrote warmly of "this grate modern Siloam, this august whirlpool ov wine, wimmin and hossis ..." (*Sayings*, 186). He describes his family of four and some eight to nine hundred other visitors drinking the mineral waters from the ten or twelve springs; and he depicts the pageantry of the annual races, the fancy buggies, the clapboard houses, and a "drove" of Indian visitors. One of the Saratoga sketches (*Ice*, 66-71) is cleverly set within a fictional frame: Shaw pretends he is on the trail of his lost Newfoundland pup and has tracked him unsuccessfully to Saratoga. Then, like Bunyan at Vanity Fair, he digresses to describe at length the scene and activities of Saratoga before ending his narrative with the disclosure that he has just heard of a lost pup turning up in New Jersey, and he will start there immediately.

Other favorite haunts Shaw wrote sketches of were Niagara Falls and, for fishing, New Ashford, Massachusetts.[11] But the area he found most relaxing and reinvigorating was the White Mountains of New Hampshire. His sketches of them are quite romantic in mood. In one (*Friend*, 575-81), he is vacationing near Mount Washington, and he finds himself completely relaxed, ebullient, and responsive to the beauties of nature. Sounding like Hawthorne in his notebook descriptions of the same area, Shaw depicts mountain scenery and emphasizes his fascination with mountains. He tells how artificial and superficial formal learning appears to him. With echoes of Wordsworth, he writes, "I kan learn more here in one week, and enjoy more, all alone with natur the skoolmarm, than I could a whole year up to my chin in the best library in the world" (*Friend*, 579)—a somewhat surprising statement from a precursor of American literary Realism.

In another sketch on the area, Shaw relates sitting on the porch of the Glen House staring vacantly at the mountain range, especially Mount Washington. He enjoys the total tranquility, wants no one to speak or even read; he desires only to sit quietly and take in the scenery. Enraptured with the sight, he exclaims that no woman has feet as pretty as the feet of mountains (*Friend*, 596); no woman has as beautiful a bust as the swelling sides of mountains (*Friend*, 597); and no man has as noble a brow as Mount Adams (*Friend*, 597). The mountains are everything he needs for complete, peaceful resuscitation, just as Long

Branch and Saratoga Springs provide escape into the excitement and gaiety of resort life.

Only occasionally does Shaw depart from geographical trends to write sketches such as "A Wimmin's League Meetin" (*Sayings*, 200-202) or "Great Agrikultural Hoss-Trott at Billingsville" (*Ice*, 42-45). He enjoyed the sketch writing, for it corresponded with his fondness for special places and pastimes. And these pieces, in turn, are generally more romantic in subject and mood than the essays. Shaw enjoyed having fun and finding relaxation in life, and the sketches often emerged from periods of recreation. Pleasant and informative pieces, they almost always contain also some note of human interest. Shaw's journalistic flair is quite evident in them, for they are the kind of article that would make brief, polished newspaper features (and that they frequently were in the columns of the *New York Weekly*).

CHAPTER 4

Salmagundi

A<small>S</small> far as short writings are concerned, Shaw's major contributions are in the forms of the aphorism, essay, and sketch;
but his columns in the *New York Weekly* and subsequently the
pages of his published books boast a wide assortment of literary
trifles such as letters to correspondents, comical narratives, situa-
tional spoofs, and even some poetry. These undertakings reveal a
man of letters with a sensitive and humanistic, if droll, approach
to life and its many situations. Shaw is an artist who could write
an hilarious prosaic parody of a newspaper advice column and
also turn out a colorful poetic description of an ice-skating scene.
His range is surprisingly broad.

I *Correspondence*

The letter as a literary type became very important to Shaw
as a result of his work for the *New York Weekly*. Being a popular
columnist and receiving abundant mail from his readers on multitudinous subjects, he soon conceived the idea of using letters
of reply—many of them fictitious—as an attractive mode of expressing his thoughts on various subjects. This mode provided
him much liberty and variety of approach, and it lent an added
personal note to his columns. Shaw found it so popular with
readers of the *Weekly* that he incorporated the letters into his
published books.

One type of letter Shaw frequently wrote is the essay-length
epistle addressed to one person, the letter form actually conceal-
ing an essay on some subject. To "Friend Elias," for example,
he relates his opinions on the military draft, sarcastically stating:
"Widder-wimmin, and their only son iz exempt, provided the

widder's husband haz alreddy sarved 2 years in the war, and iz willing tu go agin..." (*Sayings,* 35-36). The subject of "miracle" medicines provides the contents of two letters. In "Josh Billings Corresponds With a 'Hair Oil and Vegetable Bitters Man'" (*Sayings,* 209-12), Shaw compliments Doctor Hirsute on his potent hair tonic which even causes the bristles of the hairbrush to grow! The letter entitled "Billings on Pills" (*Ice,* 63-65) is a spoof of the cure-all medicine fad of his day. Josh writes Dr. Bonesett to praise his effective pills; Bonesett in turn replies that his pills cure deafness, diphtheria, baldness, headache, backsliding, and other diseases and faults.

A letter in which Shaw answers an invitation to lecture takes the form of a satire on the truth of history and its superiority to literature. The addressee is a Mr. Smith, and Shaw wonders if he is related to Captain John Smith. Shaw then recounts the John Smith-Pocahontas story but with gross errors so that his point that the "fust rate" thing about history is that "it is alwus true" is totally negated. In an important letter to Bill Davenport (*Friend,* 523-25), Shaw writes a self-analysis, enumerating his hopes, fears, habits, faith, experiences, and impressions. He concludes that he is composed of common human nature.

Other letters concern the excellence of sewing machines (*Ice,* 148-49), boyhood behavior (*Works,* 477-80), women's rights (*Works,* 483-86), and the stultifying, ultimately meaningless routines of farm labor (*Works,* 376-77): "A farmer iz the nobless work of God; he rizes at 2 o'clock in the morning, and burns out a haff a pound of wood and two kords ov kandels, and then goes out tew worry the geese and stir up the hoggs" (377).

Another type of correspondence is the letter of response to contributors—whether real or imaginary is sometimes difficult to tell—who have submitted creative work for publication in the *Weekly.* These letters appear in the columns of the *Weekly* and in Shaw's books in groups of from three to a dozen or more—most of them being short, pointed replies to the would-be authors. Shaw is often critical of the submissions. In one group of letters he tactfully but pointedly indicates plagiarism in one poem, referring to echoes of Oliver Goldsmith, Robert Burns, and Alexander Pope in its lines:

This line in your produkshun strikes us as very butiful and original; "And larn the luxury of dewing good." Gold smith [*sic*] hisself mite hav bin proud ov sich a line. And again; "Oh would sum power the gifty giv us, ov seeing oursels as uthers cee us;" yure idee ov introducing the skotch acksent into yure stile, is verry happee. If yu never hav red Robert Burns, yu will be suprised to larn that his style verry mutch resembles yures. Onse more yu sa: "If ignoranse is bliss, tis folly tew be wise." This sentiment is jist as tru as tis common. Pope, I think, has sumthing similar; but awl grate minds sometimes express theirselfs alike. (*Sayings,* 110)

In another series, Shaw attacks his contributors "at a high rate of speed" because of the inferior quality of the material (*Sayings,* 94-96). He tells them that their poetry is poor or their subject unworthy. He sometimes urges them to change to other types of writing entirely. Or he advises, "Fustly, we would sa to moste writers, 'write often, and publish seldom.' Secondly, tu sum writers, 'write seldom and publish seldemmer'" (*Sayings,* 55). In one answer Shaw has fun at the expense of prosody by writing the contributor, "I notis one ov yure lines, has 10 feet into it, and the nex one, haz only got 9 feet, six inches. . . ." And he advises this poet to practice his craft in a garret because most good poetry has "bin rit up garrett" (*Sayings,* 62-63). Finally, in one reply Shaw reveals his basis for judging poetry: "When i read a piece ov poetry that sounds so eazy, and so natral, that i wonder whi i hadn't writ sumthin like it, more than 15 years ago miself, I cum tew the konklushun, rite oph, that that iz good poetry" (*Friend,* 540-41).

The predominant type of letter in Shaw's works, however, is the letter to correspondents. As with the answers to contributors, several letters are grouped together to form a unit. These letters are in reply to innumerable inquiries concerning such subjects as Mormans, lager beer, rats, horses, fishing, music, love, family news, oil, wit and humor, dancing, rearing children, enthusiasm in religion, fashions, life in New York City, marriage, learning versus wisdom, gift distribution, Jew's harps, and hash. Many of the letters offer advice to the correspondent, some of it serious but most of it in the humorous vein. In response to an inquiry concerning the best breed of dog to buy, Shaw recommends a wooden one: they are less likely to need medical treatment, they cannot follow people away, they are quiet at night, "but if yu want one tew frighten away the robbers, awl yu hav got tew dew is tew have one made with the bark on" (*Ice,* 77).

Shaw's satiric flair occasionally turned back on himself, causing him to take a comic view of what he was doing. In one letter he burlesques the very kind of letter-answer column he was writing by penning the following befuddled reply to "Gertrude": "Yure inquiry stumps me, the darndest. The more i think on it, the more i kant tell. Az near as i kan rekolek now, i think i dont kno. Much mite be ced both ways, and neether wa be rite. Upon the whole i rather reckon i wud, or i wuddent, jist az i thought best, or otherwise" (*Sayings,* 20).

At other times, he is completely serious in his replies. On his method of thinking, he comments to one reader, "I never was logikal. I never waz a kluss kommunion thinker. I hav dun all mi thinking on the jump, i alwus shute on the wing, and hav made menny splendid misses, but once in a while hav brought down mi animal" (*Friend,* 554). And "To Jim" on the fall of man, Shaw asserts his own version of the Fortunate Fall, writing that, if man had not fallen, he would have remained lazy in Eden and never have accomplished anything. What success man has had, he opines, is due to his original fall. Ultimately, however, Shaw sees man's successes as being so minuscule and so questionable that he wonders—sounding like his friend Mark Twain—"if it wouldn't hav been just az well, when Adam waz falling, if he had fell out ov sight" (*Friend,* 554).

Several of the letters to readers concern literature. To "Byron," a hypothetical fledgling poet, Shaw warns, "Poetry is a good deal like a clothes-line, very apt tew spred lengthways if at all. Most evryʋoddy, sumtime during their lives, has the poetry ailment, jist as they hav the teeth cut, but one teeth cutting satisfies evryboddy but the phools" (*Ice,* 187). Discussing the subject of a literary reputation, he compares it to tight-rope dancing: "it takes a long time, and mutch pashunce tew git it, and it iz deuced slippery bizzness tew stand on after you hav got it" (*Friend,* 538). And he then suggests a measuring stick by which a young writer can gauge the advisability of releasing his first written work: "If yu are fully satisfied that yure fust literary effort iz perfekt, tare it up and dont be a phool but once, but if yu *sincerely* doubt its merit (which iz the hardest kind of doubt to inhale) let the publick decide between you and yure fears" (*Friend,* 538). He advises the novice not to be afraid of critics (*Friend,* 539), and he says of critics that there was never a sound one who was not a good writer himself, a fact which accounts "for the grate number ov criticks, and for the inferiority ov them" (*Friend,* 550).

In a letter to a female correspondent, Shaw comments on the nature of his own writing—particularly on its lack of sentimentalism and flamboyance:

Yu ask me whi i dont write sweet, and sentimental, and luvly things.

I aint bilt right, Caroline, for that kind ov labor.

I am tew round-shouldered, tew write perfumed sentences.

When i git hold ov an idee, i hav tew let it go out, into the world, like a bird oph from mi hand, bareheaded, and barefooted, a sort ov vagrant.

If i should undertake tew dress it up in fine clothes, sum folks would say i stole the idee, and other folks would say i tried tew steal the clothes, tew dress it in, and got ketched at it.

I make no pretentions tew literature, i pay no homage tew elegant sentences, i had rather be the father ov one genuine, original truth, i don't kare if it iz az humpbacked as a drumudary, than tew be the author ov a whole volume ov glittering cadences, gotten up, for wintergreen-eating schoolgirls tew nibble at. (*Works,* 491)

Thus the letter is a significant part of Shaw's short pieces that make up his collected works. Though not so abundant as his aphorisms and essays, the letters—whether to a contributor or correspondent or in the form of a familiar essay written to a private individual—are polished and important little exercises which further reveal Shaw's ability as a humorist and his stature as a humanist.

II   *Miscellaneous Short Pieces*

Literature was not merely Shaw's bread and butter; it was his primary amusement. Emanating from his works is the forceful personality of a self-possessed man of letters thoroughly enjoying what he is doing. Mastery and enjoyment of a skill or art often lead to experimentation, and there are a number of pieces scattered through Shaw's works that are mere trifles written for fun and variety.

The narrative mode is one that Shaw usually eschewed—one of the characteristics that distinguishes him from such fellow literary funny men as Ward, Phoenix, and Twain. Nevertheless, Shaw did experiment occasionally with narration by writing short pieces that usually involve himself or a persona as a central character. In one entitled "Narratif" (*Sayings*, 163-66), he depicts himself as a traveling pill salesman who meets a peddler of scriptures and religious tracts. Each attempts to sell the other his wares, but Shaw discovers in the course of the bargaining that the colporteur is a hypocrite—he is also a horse swapper and is really far more interested in Shaw's beast than in his soul.

Another narrative, "Josh Gits Orfully Bit" (*Sayings*, 172-73), is a fragmentary piece about Shaw's nocturnal escapade with a mouse; he had to throw a towel at the "little grey cuss" who had caused his wife to awaken screaming. Another situation, in "A Hum Transaction," finds the Billings family looking for a cook and finally settling on one who completely pleases the family with her industry and apparent knowledge of her craft until at a crucial dinner she shows her basic ignorance. Shaw comments, "If 'ignorance iz bliss,' Irish cooks must be the verry broth ov happiness" (*Ice*, 163).

In "A True Fish Story Founded on Fak," Shaw relates a story about two western preachers, a Baptist and a Methodist, who held baptismal services at a local pond on Wednesdays and Saturdays, respectively. On one Wednesday the Methodist observes the Baptist's services and notices that, among those being baptized, are several that he himself had scheduled for his Saturday ritual. When he meets the Baptist the following day and accuses him of the "pious fraud," the Baptist gleefully retorts, "Brother Sturgiss, mi father larnt me when i was but a little fisher-boy, tew string mi fish as fast as i ketched 'em" (*Sayings*, 204).

A satirical narrative entitled "The Muggins Family" spoofs the growing tendency of post-Civil War Americans to journey to Europe and shows how too often those Americans, with their pedestrian tastes and backgrounds and pretentious airs, are essentially incapable of profiting from their experiences—a satiric picture of what Henry James often presented seriously:

Silvester Muggins haz gone tew Yewrupp.

He left in the Kunard line.

The recent rize in cheeze so inflated him and hiz pocket book, that it waz wuss than madness for him tew stay on this side ov the atlantick oshun enny longer.

He took all hiz live traps with him, which konsisted ov one wife, two dauters, hiz only son Reuben, and a lap dog bought for the ockashun.

They took a fust-class passage; one hundred dollars in gold each, the dog throne in.

He will make the tower of Yewrupp, meandering through Skotland, Ingland, and Ireland; then krossing into France he will pennetrate thru that kingdum, bi the aid of gide books, from thence he will investigate into Jermany and Switzerland, and will see Naples if it kills him and the rest ov the family.

Silvester Muggins and troupe hav never bin from home before, the cheeze faktory haz absorbed their time and genius till now, and they expekt tew cum bak eddikated and hily polished.

The two dauters will hav a French and Jerman nurse at once, and they are tew be teached how tew do and say things ov a forrin natur, if it kosts 2 thousand dollars tew do it.

Silvester Muggins sed this before he set sail.

Mrs. Muggins iz a leetle too old and tuff to shine up mutch, but they will dress her and not let her talk mutch, so it iz reported.

Old Muggins himself dont expekt to polish, he iz too cheezy, he will pay the bills, and sample forrin curds.

Reuben Muggins will enter sum Jerman skool, and will be put thru for 3 years, to the tune of "root hog or die," for Silvester, his fater sed so, just before he sailed.

Silvester Muggins iz solemly determined that his sprout Reuben shall know learning, and be forever abuv the cheeze bizzness.

The 2 dauters will cum bak in 3 years from now, and hav thirteen nu silk dresses each to sho, also a kammill's hare shawl, and fourteen boxes ov gluvs, and tork sum Jerman and French at the table when they want sum more hash, or want the pertataze passed.

The lap dorg, i don't kno what will bekum ov him; it may not be the phashion over thare tew tote lap dorgs; if it ain't, the dear konfiding purp will be dropt.

Silvester Muggins haz stuk tew cheeze for 34 years kluss, and don't kno enny thing about hiz natiff land.

He kan't tell whitch way the Mississippi River runs, nor don't kno whitch State the Falls ov Niagara are situated in.

If enny boddy over in old imperial Rome should ask Silvester Muggins if Keokuk waz lokated on the Tombigbee he would hav tew say yes, or admit he had forgot.

He knoze a grate deal more about the uplands in Switzerland than he duz about the rizing ground in Nu Hamshire, bekauze he and the whole family hav bin wrapt in forrin gide books for the last 6 months, nite and day.

If enny boddy over in Paris should pass the Mugginses enny cheeze at the table yu would hear them all say "horrid!" except Silvester, and he would ask the lackey on the sli if it was skim or nu milk.

The family kan't bear the smel ov cheese now.

When the Muggins family cum bak three years from now, they will pretty mutch hav forgot their natiff tung, all except the old man and the old woman.

The whole family will forgit their nabors, and won't be able tew enjoy enny thing nor talk enny thing but Yewripp.

Silvester, and the old woman, will probably go at cheeze agin, but the rest ov the troupe will be too polished, and spilte, for the skim cheeze bizzness.

Silvester is not a bad man at all, when he iz around the cheeze faktory, he haint got mutch branes it iz trew, but the late rize in cheeze dislokated him, and the family ketched the sudden Yewripp disorder, and giv it tew him, and it haz made the whole ov them ridikilus.

The 2 dauters when they cum bak, will simply be silly.

Ruben wont kno enny thing, but this waz alwuss natral tew him.

The old woman will make hash ov things aufully, she will tell her nabors all about the leaning tower of Copenhagen, and the Pantheon ov Paris, and the bridge ov sighs at Dublin, and evry now and then will risk a french or jerman phraze, which will be decidedly cheezy.

The Muggins never ought tew have gone abroad at all, they were industrious here, and tharefore kimparatively respektabel, they are ritch and unkultivated now, and are in Yewripp.

They are being laffed at bi the refined, and cheated by the unskrupulus.

Thare are thousands ov the Muggins Amerikans now on the opposite side ov the atlantik oshun, and thousands more will go, for

it iz generally understood bi the Muggins class that if yu haint bin
tew Yewripp, yu aint mutch.

The well bred find no difference, tew speak on, between the well
bred ov Yewripp and the well bred at hum, but the snobs do.

Snobs vary ackordin tew latitude and longitude, and ours go
abroad tew inkrease their average.[1]

Shaw even created one little dramatic piece, a burlesque of
the theater. Entitled "A Tablows in 4 Acks," the work is quite
representative of Shaw's satiric humor, as he depicts ridiculous
slapstick antics on the stage:

Ack Fust.—Enter a lap dorg, carrying a boarding skool miss in
his arms, about 16 hands high—it makes the dorg puff—the dorg
lays down the boarding skool miss, and orders mint juleks for 2,
with the usual suckshun. The dorg begins tew loll, the boarding
skool miss tells him "tew dri up," (in French,) and the dorg sez
"he be darned if he will," (in Dorg) [Grate sensashun among the
awjence, with cries, "put him out!"] Finally a compromize iz affected,
the boarding skool miss kisses the dorg, with tears in his eyes.
Konlusion—Lap dorg diskovers a wicked flee at work on his tale—
pursues him—round and round tha go—dorg a leettle ahead—sumbody hollers out, "mad dorg!"—boarding skool girl faints standing—
the curtin drops.

Ack number 2.—Curtin highsts—sevral blind men in the distanse,
looking thru a key whole—one ov them sez, "he don't see it!" A
shanghi ruseter cums out, with epaulets on, and crows Yankee
Doodle—musik bi the band. The shanghi lays an egg on the stage,
about the size ov a wasps nest, and then limps oph, very much
tired and redused. Curtin falls agin.

Ack number 3.—Curtin rizes sloly—big bolona sarsage on a tabel—
bolona sarsage lifts up her hed, and begins tew bark—band plays
"Old Dorg Tray." Cat cums in—cat's tail begins tew swell bad—
bolona sarsage and cat haz a fite—tha fite 14 rounds—the stage iz
covered with cats and dorgs. Konlusion—tha awl jine hands, and
walk tew the foot lights—an old Bull Tarrier reads the President's
call for "300,000 more"—band plays "Go in Lemons!"—a bell rings,
and the curtin drops

Ack number 4.—A scene on the Eri kanall—a terribel storm rages—
the kanall acks bad—sevral line botes go down hed fust, with awl
their boarders on board—kant make a lee shore—tha drag their
ankers—sum ov the kaptins tri tew pra, but moste ov them have the
best luck at swareing—the water iz strewed with pots and kittles—

sevral ov the cook maids swim ashore, with their cook stoves in their teeth—tha hav tew draw oph the kanal tew stop the storm. Konlusion —men are seen along on the banks ov the kanall spearing ded hosses and eels—band plays "a life on the oshun wave." Amid tremduous applauze the curtin falls, and the awjence disperce, single file. (*Sayings,* 22-24)

Perhaps on the circuit between lectures or in his playgoing in New York Shaw had experienced nights of boredom or inanity in the theater, and this piece was a method of seeking revenge. The burlesque is remindful in places of "The King's Came-leopard, or The Royal Nonesuch" in *Huckleberry Finn.* Shaw, along with Twain, had seen audiences subjected to senseless antics on the stage, and he was largely disillusioned with the theater.

Among other burlesques, Shaw wrote a delightful satirical trifle on feminist movements entitled "The Zantippee," a spoof that reflects his criticism of women's stand. Some echoes of the "new feminism" of the second half of the twentieth century are sounded in many of the articles of the Zantippee charter:

The Zantippee iz an orginashun ov fearless and stought minded wimmin in New York citty, the purposes and intent ov which iz fully set forth in the following by-laws and resolushuns, found lately at a pawn-broker's shop in the pocket ov a pair of cassimere femail unspeakabels:

Artikle 1st. This confederacy shall be called the Zantippee, and shall be perpetual and everlasting.

2. It shall be compozed entirely ov femails, nothing ov the male natur shall be allowed within ten miles ov it.

3. Every member ov this club shall have an offiss, provided they are sound on the goose and down on the gander.

4. No married woman shall be admitted tew this club who duz not wear a full suit ov cassimere at home.

5. This assosiation iz self-lifting, and don't ask enny odds ov the male kritters.

6. Resolved, that we will vote or smash the ballot-boxes ov creashun.

7. No woman shall be deemed iligible tew offiss who iz afrade ov enny man living.

8. Young girls between the ages ov twenty-five and thirty received on trial.

9. The objekt ov this confederacy iz tew do away with the necessity ov mankind and exalt woman tew her treu sphear, and enable her tew run the concern hereafter forevermore in good shape.

10. Good moral karakter requisite for admishun tew this club, but too much beauty shall be deemed a leetle risky, and shall be watched by a committee ov five grown females from among the elders with power tew report from time tew time whether the new member is sound on the voting question, and the right tew set onto jurys.

11. Resolved, that we won't pay enny more taxes, nor git enny more breakfast (be darned if we do) if we kant hav sum femail suffrage.

12. Resolved, if we don't look out the niggers will get tew voting before we do.

13. No member of this confederacy shall be liable tew arrest for slander, or pulling hair, or enny thing aginst the so-called stattues ov the country, while they are in session.

14. Enny male being caught within the sakred precincts ov Zantippee, on enny pretence whatever, shall be beheaded with a ruffled nightcap and be drummed out ov the camp. *Provided* nothing in this artikle shall be so construed az to interfere with a marrid man's bringing into an antercom an infant ov the femail kind, whose preservashun depends upon the ministering cumforts ov the mother ov the child, the mother at the time being aktually present, at a regular organized meeting ov the confederacy.

15. No looking glasses allowed in the senate chamber of Zantippee —no New York *Herald* allowed—no demokratick paper ov enny kind allowed, and all the proceedings ov the club tew be kept az sekret az possibel, under the cercumstansis ov the case.

16. In case enny ov the proceedings ov the club are divulged tew an outside femail friend, it iz distinktly understood, that said femail friend, iz to divulge the same only tew her most intimate friend, and then only upon express condishun, that said intimate friend iz tew do the same, under penalty ov the law, made, and provided for sich cases.

17. No femail, in love, will be permitted tew bekum a member ov the confederacy, but all such femails shall hav the simpathy ov the club, for human natur we know iz tuff tew fite with.

18. No lap-dorgs, nor yung ones, nor knitting, nor house-wife talking, nor receipts for cooking, allowed on the premises.

19. Resolved, If enny member ov the Zantippee iz sent for by her husband during bizzness hours, she needn't pay enny attenshun tew the critter, but for a handsum speech upon the occashun, defining

wimmin's rights, and defying man and hiz course attributes, she shall be rewarded with a vote of thanks, and a copy ov the bye-laws and resolushuns ov the club.

20. All singly blessed members ov the confederacy, who hav stood firm aginst the blarney ov men, tew enter the so-called wedded state, shall each carry a golden spear during session, emblematick ov their heroism, in defending their charms against the highway robbers ov wimmin's rights.

21. Resolved, if enny member ov the association iz seized with a desire for matrimony, while under the fostering auspices ov the association, and can't be healed ov the disseaze, we will weep over her, and attend the wedding, az a tribute ov respekt for our female sister.

22. The Zantippee reserves the privilege ov altering enny ov the above resolushuns, bye-laws, or edikts, and adding from time tew time others, that the welfair ov the club may demand. (*Weekly,* July 29, 1869, p. 4)

As a professional realtor, Shaw was, of course, well versed in the art of advertising. Having some sport with his own profession, he wrote several burlesque advertisements that mock the stock devices of the realtor's word game. One spectacular estate is described in language that exceeds hyperbole:

ADVERTIZEMENT

I kan sell for eighteen hundred and thirty-nine dollars, a pallas, a sweet and pensive retirement, lokated on the virgin banks ov the Hudson, kontaining 85 acres. The land is luxuriously divided by the hand of natur and art, into pastor and tillage, into plain and deklivity, into stern abruptness, and the dallianse ov moss-tufted medder; streams ov sparkling gladness, (thick with trout,) danse through this wilderness ov buty, tew the low musik ov the kricket and grasshopper. The evergreen sighs az the evening zephir flits through its shadowy buzzum, and the aspen trembles like the luv-smitten harte ov a damsell. Fruits ov the tropicks, in golden buty, melt on the bows, and the bees go heavy and sweet from the fields to their garnering hives. The manshun iz ov Parian marble, the porch iz a single diamond, set with rubiz and the mother ov pearl; the floors are ov rosewood, and the ceilings are more butiful than the starry vault of heavin. Hot and cold water bubbles and squirts in evry apartment, and nothing is wanting that a poet could pra for, or art could portray. The stables are worthy of the steeds ov Nimrod or the studs ov Akilles, and its henery waz bilt expressly

for the birds ov paradice; while somber in the distance, like the
cave ov a hermit, glimpses are caught ov the dorg-house. Here poets
hav cum and warbled their laze—here skulptors hav cut, here painters
hav robbed the scene ov dreamy landskapes, and here the philosopher
diskovered the stun, which made him the alkimist ov natur. Nex
northward ov this thing ov buty, sleeps the residense and domain
ov the Duke John Smith; while southward, and nearer the spice-
breathing tropicks, may be seen the barronial villy ov Earl Brown,
and the Duchess, Widder Betsy Stevens. Walls ov primitiff rock,
laid in Roman cement, bound the estate, while upward and down-
ward, the eye catches far away, the magesta and slow grander ov
the Hudson. As the young morn hangs like a cutting ov silver
from the blu brest ov the ski, an angel may be seen each night
dansing with golden tiptoes on the green. (N.B. This angel goes
with the place.)

Biagrams kan be seen at the offiss ov the broker. Terms flattering.
None but principals delt with. Title as pure as the breth ov a white
male infant, and possession given with the lark. For more full
deskripshun, read Ovid's Art ov Luv, or kall (in yure carriage) on
Josh Billings, Real Estate Agent. (*Sayings*, 193-95)

Another realty advertisement spoofs terms of agreement, with
Josh driving an incredibly hard bargain. Concerning one of the
houses advertised, he writes:

To a tenant who kan bring testimony, and a good pedigree, this
hous would be leased for a term ov 30 or 40 years, for about 2,500
hundred dollars a year, the tenant tew pay the taxes, and remove
the mortgages now on the premises, and put in the gass, and git
the hous insured for 6,000 dollars, and assign the polisy tew the
agent az collatteral security for the faithful performanse ov the
kontrakt. N.B.—If thare iz enny things else that i hav forgot tew
menshun about the terms, the tennant kan hav them inserted, when
the papers are drawed up, without extra charge. (*Ice*, 81)

The prospects for the leasee of a second dwelling are hardly
better:

This delightful property iz now occupied bi a phisician, ("whose
sands ov life hav about run out,") and sum ov the rent would be
took in boarding the phisician ("whose sand iz about run thru,")
and hiz wife, and wife's oldest sister, and her unkle, and the 9

children, who are awl lite eaters, havin bin kept for the laste 6 months on sperm kandle soup. Tew a tenant who could loan the phisician $1,500 or two thousand dollars, and take a first mortgage on the furniture in the hous, a liberal rent would be named, payable quarterly in advanse. P.S.—fust cum, fust git. (*Ice,* 81-82)

The verbal chicanery continues. One house is listed as a "Gothick Cottage, (with chimbleys, and windo blinds attached,) and water, (in the suller,) ...," and it "kontains a bay windo; would suit a lawyer or a blacksmith" (*Ice,* 80). Another residence "is a cross ov the Ionian & Dorick style, waz built when lumber was skarse, and iz almitey hard finished throughout, ratholes awl plugged up, and a bottle ov bed bugg pizen, neatly labeled, and hung up in each room" (*Ice,* 81). Shaw wants no foolishness from interested parties: "No children and doggs aloud on the premises. Cards, tew view the hous, kan be obtained ov the agent (admitting a gentleman and 2 ladys) for the trifling sum ov 5 dollars" (*Ice,* 80). To the exasperation of any interested party having read an advertisement through carefully, Shaw adds a note to the bottom of one advertisement: "N.B.— This hous waz taken yesterday, and customers are forbid tew bother the agent bi inquiring about it" (*Ice,* 80).

Finally, Shaw included some speeches by Josh Billings in his works. These exercises are often sententious or instructional in nature. In an address to the "Femail Billingsville Sowing Society," Josh states that his heart is warmed by the ladies' sewing for charity; and he commends their industry and faithfulness in their work. He encourages them to persevere in their calling, despite criticism from "the ritch and the hawty": "Stan bi yure konstitushion, and bi laws, dew aul this, and the 'Femail Billingsville Sowing Society' will go down tew futer prosterita, like a wide-awake torchlite possession" (*Sayings,* 46). In "A Lekture to Male Young Men Only," he offers advice to young men just starting out in life, telling them to mull over carefully what their callings are to be so that they will determine with assurance that they are dedicating their lives to the right vocations. His concluding remarks are: "If you foller the direckshuns laid down above, yu will diskiver the wigglings ov yure genius, in time perhaps, tew saive yureselfs from cuming the governor ov sum

state, when natur kindly ramified yu for a carpenter and jiner"
(*Sayings*, 89).

III *Poetry*

Occasionally Shaw wrote poetry that appeared in his *Weekly*
column, major works, and jest books. The ten volumes of the
Allminax have quatrains of verse at the tops of most of the calendar pages, and there is poetry in Shaw's jest book *Josh Billings'*
Spice Box (though, granted, most of it is probably merely
selected, not written, by him). His longest and best poem is an
effective little narrative on fishing entitled "Sum Very Blank
Verse—The Negro and the Trout."[2] The descriptive and colorful
introduction demonstrates Shaw's own love of the outdoors, and
it also echoes the nature poetry of the Thomson-Pope tradition.
The tone, in fact, is quite eighteenth century:

> Beneath the shelvy bank ov meddo brook,
> Expektant lays the spekeld trout.
> April showers, with blood from
> Genial skize, have warmed the streamlet's
> Veins, and dancing on its buzzum
> Cums sunlite and shaddo
> Hand in hand.
> Just here the verdant willow bends,
> To lave its tapring fingers
> In the kristal flood,
> And fragrant spearmint scents the
> Creeping wind.
> Close by, upon the alders highest limb
> Swaying, the blackbird sits,
> With mello thrut full ov April songs,
> Responsiv tew the sadder notes
> Of Robin red breast from yonder maple,
> While sollum az phuneral cortege
> The dusky crow beats his wing
> Against the swimming ski.
> 'Tis Spring! or from the brooklet's
> Grassy bank the violets would not
> Be stareing with their eyes ov
> Gentle blue, nor in the smoky air
> Would indistinkt be heard

The thousand echo's waking,
Half dreaming, from their frozen sleep.
Sweet time! the yung year innocent.
Gentle Spring! in undress,
Unconscious ov her buty, spreds
Her golden tresses to the wanton wind,
While buds and blossoms early
Welkum the lovely goddess to
This throne of hers,
And reddy stand, with harps soft strung,
With dreamy musik,
Sweet time! ov all the varied year,
Most charming and oftnest sung.

Following these lines, the poem introduces the Negro fisher-
man in a vivid descriptive picture and creates a mood of excitement and expectancy as he places his line in the water and
awaits the trout:

In menny a looped and squirming
Knott he hangs the hook about,
With fresh and tempting worms.
One step nearer—still one more—
Then waving in the air aloft
The flexile line, and light,
With hand unerring, the pole
Obedient drops the struggling
Worm just in the current's mouth,
Whare the water fust begins its race.
Oh! art exquisitt! Oh! bliss extatic!—

The catch comes appropriately at the height of the poem's
crescendo, and Shaw's own enthusiasm cannot be contained:

Down the brook's swift thrut swims
The giddy worm, a fatal journey,
For darting, az a streak ov silvry light
From sentinal place, the
Spekled gourmand burys in hiz maw
The barbed deceit.
Now who kan tell, with words enuff,
The thrill that follows?

       I kant!
       But stranger look! upon the grassy
       Bank, dancing in deth, and see a
       Two Pound trout, game and butiful
       To the last.

The poem is surprisingly well written from standpoints of imagery, description, balance, mood, and total effect. Even the flexible, if unorthodox, metrical pattern seems perfectly in order as it establishes a rhythm hovering between blank and free verse. One wishes only that Shaw had written more like it.

Much of the flavor and variety of Shaw's talent, thus, is made apparent by the copious miscellaneous short pieces. In the letter and other bagatelles, he displayed his versatile interests. He often experimented with modes he considered basically foreign to his pen, such as poetry and narration; and his success with them brings regret that he did not do more. He had definite talent in those areas. It was Shaw's twofold purpose as a writer to be both instructional and entertaining. In most of these minor pieces he was concentrating on entertainment.

CHAPTER 5

Jest Books

B ESIDES his regular hardbound volumes, Henry Wheeler
Shaw published several paperbound jest books.[1] The jest
book—a form that emerged in England during the Renaissance,
became especially popular there in the eighteenth century and
proliferated in America in the nineteenth—is, as Harry B. Weiss
defines the genre, "the cheap, paper-covered, joke books that
were, and still are, printed in large editions for sale to the
general public, usually for comparatively small sums of money."[2]
The term *jest book* carries with it no particular specifications as
far as contents are concerned; "jests" can be literally jokes, or
epigrams, anecdotes, humorous almanac entries, ludicrous illus-
strations, and repartee (with frequent puns). Though not a
requirement, the humor can be enhanced by any number of
devices such as misspellings, exaggerations, incorrect grammar,
and anticlimax.[3] In short, as long as a work was a brief, inex-
pensive paperback containing an assortment of humorous material, it could be classified as a jest book.

The popularity of jest books during Shaw's day was augmented
by the rise of comic periodicals and by the increasing number
of humorous newspaper and magazine columns during the last
half of the nineteenth century.[4] This flourish of humorous journalism played into Shaw's hands as he mulled over the type of
material most suitable for jest book form.

I Ansestrals Sighns

Shaw's first offering in the jest book tradition was a reprint
of *Josh Billings' Farmer's Allminax* for 1874, published under
the title *Twelve Ansestrals Sighns in the Billings' Zodiac Gallery*

(1873). A slender volume of thirty pages, it begins satirically with introductory material consisting of a title page which spoofs the Man of the Signs diagram (see Chapter 6); a page of inane "Sighns and Wonders For the Year 1874" ("Whenever yu see an old goose setting on a post hole, and trieing tew hatch the hole out, yu kan cum tew the konklushun that she is strikly a one idee goose" [4]); and a page of humorous blurbs for *Josh Billings' Allminax*. Sandwiched between this frontal material and the conclusion, which is also a page of jests, are the twelve almanac calendar pages and, on the facing pages, twelve clever genealogical essays on Billings' ancestors. Each of these facing pages ends with a witty moral.

Since the composition of Shaw's humorous calendar pages is discussed in Chapter 6, attention here is devoted to the genealogies. Twelve members of the "Billings family" and their personal traits are presented, the family line sporting a colorful collection of names—some biblical (the list suggesting the lengthy genealogies of the Old Testament) and some comically fanciful. The twelve are Adam, Zepheniah, Jehossaphatt, Melkisidek, Solomon, Duteronomy, Porkanbeans, Jamaika, Ekleeziastiks, Luke, Nebudkennezzar, and Mushanmilk.

The first of the Billingses was Adam, who was born "about the year 1200" and "waz named after the original Adam" (6). Unmindful of his progenerative powers, "little did he dream ov the glorious krop that waz a going tew spring up from hiz sowing." His major accomplishments were dancing and "bending" the truth: "He was too fond ov the marvelous, he wouldn't tell a lie exackly, but he could cum az near tew it, as a swallo kan to a frog's noze, when they skim a mud puddle."

It soon becomes evident that Adam's questionable habits established a paradigm for all his descendants. Each one, though usually talented in some way, possessed some major character flaw. Zepheniah was a good fiddler but was always in debt to people (8); Jehossaphatt was stingy (10); Melkisidek was too arduous a lover of "the whole entire femail populashun" (12); Soloman, despite his wisdom, had "a grate deal ov vanity, a large amount ov impudense, a good supply ov inkredulity..." (14); Jamaika Billings was "the lazyest man that ever visited this world" (20); and such traits continue through the remaining family members. Looking back on this troupe of ancestors, Josh decides that "they were rather a thin set"; and in what surely amounts to a humorous view of the sins of the fathers concept, he concludes: "I find that their *ambishun* waz the result of *vanity*. Their *honesty* the effekt ov *edukashun*. Their *charity*, the luv ov *novelty*. Their *philosophy*, able tew bear the stummukake ov others with heroik fortitude, but not worth a kuss in their own; and their *virteus* generally, more the growth ov their *pride* than ov their *humility*. What a pitty! Echo answers, 'Jiss so.' Man iz an angleworm. He iz. Verily" (28).

The short morals following the character sketches have no bearing on the family members described. These morals, in the form of jingles, add humor to the book with such observations as:

> The klussest man i ever knu,
>   Waz Deakon Erastus Meggs,
> Tew save expense, he oft would sett,
>   Hiz pullets on spile-ed eggs.   (10)

> Wisdum chunks are chunkier far,
> Than all the chunks that chunky ar.   (14)

> Tew swop a horse and not git beat,
>   Iz sumthing nice tew brag on,
> I tried it once, and that's the time
>   I lost a horse—and waggon.   (18)

> I never knu, in all mi life, ,
>   Enny man tew go krazy,
> Who alwuss took things setting down,
>   And kultivated hiz lazy.   (20)

> Evry man thinks he kan keep a hotel,
>   But O! how delusiv and rash,
> For thare aint no kind ov bizzness so mixt,
>   Az doing a klean job in hash.   (26)

The predominant approach, then, in *Twelve Ansestrals Sighns*, is that of satire and burlesque, an approach Shaw used in a later jest book, the *Cook Book*. Though in some ways it cannot rank as a separate original production—since it is a reprint—it was quite important to Shaw's career in that it awakened his interest in jest books and prompted him to do others which did have quite original and varied formats.

II Spice Box

The lengthiest and most diverse of Shaw's jest books were the volumes he edited under the series title *Josh Billings' Spice Box* (1874 and following),[5] a title Shaw borrowed from his *New York Weekly* column. Printed with sometimes as many as fifty large double-column pages[6] and occasionally selling for as high as twenty-five cents, each of these volumes offers as much material as his other jest books combined. They are veritable potpourris of illustrations, cartoons, jokes, poems, anecdotes, narratives, letters, and other short pieces—works designed primarily for browsing. A major difference between *Spice Box* and Shaw's other jest books is that much of its material is only collected and edited by Shaw, not written by him.

The *Spice Box* volumes are the most richly illustrated of all Shaw's jest books. The drawings—almost all of them anonymous[7]—are perhaps the most prominent and engrossing feature, serving a far more functional role in the humor of the work than do those illustrations in the other books. The very title page of the issue by J. S. Ogilvie is symbolically adorned with the caricature of a smiling gargantuan figure, who resembles both Josh Billings and Uncle Sam, scattering grains of spices from a pan labeled "Rich and Rare" to an enthusiastic crowd of receivers gathered about his feet. The inside dedication carries out the cover motif by proclaiming, "This little waif is most respectfully dedicated to the millions of people who love wit and humor, and to the rest of creation besides—upon receipt of price." The body of the work itself contains some eighty-seven humorous illustrations, seventeen of them being half a page in size. The other seventy are of varying sizes, usually a column in width and about three inches high, so that four can appear on a page (one in each corner) and leave ample space for text.

The majority of the illustrations are individual cartoons, such as the one that shows two obese gentlemen literally standing paunch to paunch, the caption reading "Extremes Meet" (6).

Others, however, depart from the single incident and—in the only instances of this nature in all of Shaw's works—appear in related groups or sequences. One group of four cartoons, for example, punningly illustrate common sayings or phrases: a picture of a determined-looking mother thrusting her child in bed is labeled "A Mad Donna and Child"; that of a naughty schoolboy being yanked up by the hair by his master is called "Son Rise— By an Old Master"; a young lady surrounded by suitors is "The Dear at Bay"; and the sale of a reduced vest at Abraham's second-hand clothing shop is labeled "Abraham's Sacrifice" (29). *Spice Box* (still the Ogilvie issue) also contains cartoon serials, resembling newspaper comic strips, that run from two to three pages in length.

There are many other assorted "spices" in these collections besides illustrations. There is a preponderance of funny anecdotes. There are also jokes and witty sayings; humorous quotations; clever letters to and from contributors and correspondents (these undoubtedly written by Shaw himself); riddles ("What kind of essence does a young man like when he pops the question?" "Acquiescense" [Ogilvie, 29]); and brief space fillers that tell of quaint customs, laws, or events. Conspicuous by their absence are the usual essays which are replaced by the numerous anecdotes that relate a multitude of humorous situations.

All in all, the *Spice Box* volumes are probably Shaw's most genuinely entertaining jest books. Unlike some of the others, their pages are uncluttered by prolific advertising, having only the customary publishing-house promotion pages. Every one of the sizable pages offers a sparkling variety of humorous odds and ends. Presented mostly in normal spelling, grammar, and syntax, these books are the most likely of all Shaw's jest books to provide an evening's curious entertainment for the modern reader.

III   Trump Kards

Next came *Josh Billings' Trump Kards: Blue Grass Philosophy* (1877), a forty-six-page volume containing twelve full-page illustrations by F. S. Church.[8] Underscoring the title of the volume, the title page depicts a small extended hand holding five

cards, and an underlying inscription reads: "The time to be
karefullest iz when yu hav a hand full ov trumps. =Yures 'til
deth. Josh Billings." Shaw dedicated the book to his grandchil-
dren: "three sweet little tyrants, who kan make their Grandpa
akt like a phool enny time they hav a mind to." Following are
sixteen essays and sketches, upwards of twenty pages of witty
aphorisms, illustrations, and—in the end pages—advertisements
of New York firms selling insurance, safes and scales, household
cleaner, tobacco, men's clothing, tooth powder, carriages, and
other goods. Included is an advertisement for Street and Smith's
New York Weekly, billed as "The leading Story and Sketch paper
of the age." Advertising was not a common practice in jest books;[9]
yet Shaw used it copiously in both *Trump Kards* and *Struggling
With Things*.

The essays and sketches in *Trump Kards*—most of them one
page in length—are as diverse as others in Shaw's books. There
is one on grandfathers which assesses their contributions, shortcomings, and general traits; a panegyric on "Pork and Beans"
somewhat remindful—though in prose—of Joel Barlow's *The
Hasty Pudding* ("I sing ov Pork and Beans. All hail! yee greasy,
and helth inspiring bulbs" [11]); a glimpse of the burdensome
life of a country schoolboy; a clever essay on "Pets" (covering all
types from pet dogs, to pet children, to pet ideas and hobbies);
a reflection on youthful prankishness entitled "When I Waz
a Boy"; a descriptive account of "Lager Beer, and Spruce
Gum"; typical Shaw animal essays on "The Ram, and Craw-
fish"; sketches on Long Branch, "The Mermaid," and country
sausage; a biographical sketch of one "Job Pierson"; and short
pieces on "A Ghost" and "Hash." Also included are a shortened
version of "The Muggins Family," the satire on European
travel written earlier for the *New York Weekly* (see Chapter 4)
and a letter to one "Butiful Brown" in which Shaw reveals much
about his own habits, beliefs, and personal life (see Chapter 1).

An added attraction to the volume is that most of the essays
and sketches are immediately preceded by one of Church's full-
page illustrations highlighting the subject of the essay. Thus,
the "Mermaid" sketch is introduced by a woodcut of a mermaid
reclining on a rock under a smiling sun and admiring herself
in a hand mirror, while three penguins and a stork look on

(30). Undoubtedly the most original illustration, prefixed to the essay "Hash," shows a farm wife turning the handle of the "Hash Machine" while a personified pig, rooster, ram, potato, fish, brace of ducks, and other potential "ingredients" wait dourly in line to be ground up and spewed from the back of the machine into a bucket (42). The illustrations are in keeping with the general tendency in the jest books to illustrate copiously. In *Trump Kards*, however, they are more directly related to the prose pieces than are most illustrations in Shaw's other jest books.

<h2 style="text-align:center">IV Cook Book</h2>

An obscure work not generally known to be a part of the Shaw canon is *Josh Billings' Cook Book and Picktorial Proverbs* (1880),[10] a slender, twenty-four-page book underwritten by, and dedicated to, Caswell, Hazard & Co., Druggists and Chemists, a firm supplying the only advertising to appear in the volume.

Unlike the jest books considered thus far, the format of each page of *Cook Book* is the same. At the top is an aphorism, then a comic illustration[11] with accompanying caption—all these items consuming almost half the page. Then comes the humorous recipe or other item appearing in one paragraph, followed at the bottom of the page by another aphorism. Each unit on the page is independent in subject matter of the others. The two aphorisms at top and bottom have nothing to do with each other nor with either the illustration or recipe. Nor are the illustration and the recipe related. Moreover, nothing but the recipe itself has anything to do with the subject of food.

In a letter "To the Dear Publick" which serves as a preface, Josh informs his gourmands that these recipes "are the suggestions ov a man who never haz been able to cook hiz own goose just exactly right." But he assures his readers "that they are submitted . . . by one, who haz but little malice in hiz natur, and less cunning." Should his hints not produce culinary perfection, Josh consoles his friends with the thought, "Just thank the Lord they aint enny wuss than they are, and yu hav gained sumthing bi the experiment" (3).

There are thirteen recipes in all, pertaining to such dishes as

cranberry pie, roast goose, deviled crabs, hash,[12] fried eels, dough-
nuts, and rye coffee. One of Shaw's more exotic and improbable
morsels is described in the recipe for shadow soup:

Pik out a good thin chicken (Shanghi breed iz the best), disrobe
him ov hiz plumage, amputate his spurs, remove the comb from
hiz hed, konfiscate hiz tale feathers, place him in a strong sunlight,
let the shaddo reach akrost two gallons ov strained rain water in a
shallow pan, let the shaddo remain on the water for 10 minnitts,
then take him bi the bill, and lead him gently backwards and
forwards through the water, three or four times, bring the water
to a sudden boil, seazon to suit the taste, and serve up with a raw
onion, and a bunch ov wooden tooth-picks. This soup iz very popular
with boarding-house keepers, and it iz sed, will kure the dispepshee,
or kill the patient, I hav forgot whitch. (9)

Pages not containing recipes are devoted to correspondence
(Josh answers questions concerning the recipes he has given)
and other items such as a catalogue giving dates in history when
certain dishes were first prepared, and a ballad of the "Noble
Kodphish Ball":

Cum listen to mi story, yee men and wimmin all,
While I sing to yu a ditty ov the *Noble Kodfish Ball.*
Korn beef and cabbage haz its friends, and so haz suckertash,
And sum there be who relish, a plate ov mutton hash.
Baked beans and pork are well enuff, but since poor Adam's fall,
Nothing has diskounted yet, a boneless kodfish ball.
Let Britons praze roast beef, and Frenchmen frogs hind leggs,
And Germans sing ov sassages, and beer in little kegs,
The universal Yanke nashun, her lads and lasses all,
Will ever shout the prazes ov, the *Noble Kodfish Ball.*

At the end of *Cook Book,* after he has offered his best tips
about the various dishes, Josh explains in his "Konklushuns"
that—having eaten all manner of prepared foods, dined in all
sorts of eating places, having "studded bills of fare, untill I lost
mi appetight in a labarinth ov mizerable French"—he has come
to agree with the old proverb that "The Lord sends us meat,
and the Devil sends us cooks" (22). These thirteen ludicrous
recipes assuredly had no part in correcting the gist of that adage,
but they certainly must have supplied many humorous moments

of reading to successful and unsuccessful cooks alike. It is a most entertaining little volume.

V Struggling With Things

The year 1881 brought the least literary and most rudimentary of Shaw's jest books—*Josh Billings Struggling With Things*. The oddity of this twenty-three-page pamphlet is that it exists primarily for the sake of the advertising which dominates its pages. Like the *Cook Book*, each page begins with an aphorism, followed by an illustration[13] and accompanying aphorism-caption, all of these constituting almost half a page. Then, in very pronounced type, an advertisement for a firm consumes nearly the remainder of the page, the only other material being a lone aphorism concluding each page.

The illustrated aphorisms are similar to most of Shaw's—philosophical observations, lessons about life, restatements of basic truths. A typical one shows a mule jumping a rail fence, the caption reading, "Mules are like sum men, to git them whare yu want them, turn them into the lot jineing, and let them jump out" (16). Another shows a little man astride a running pig; the man has lopped off the animal's tail and is attempting to blow through it. The caption warns, "Yu kan make a whissell out ov a pig's tale, but yu will spile a decent-looking tale, and get a kursid poor whissell" (15). As with the *Cook Book*, the aphorisms at tops and bottoms of the pages are unrelated to the illustrations or to each other.

The advertisements range over such concerns as dry goods, men's clothing, tramway cars, hotels, pianos, fishing tackle, Street & Smith's *New York Weekly*, fine silk umbrellas, carriages, banks, and insurance. At one point, Shaw advertises himself by reproducing one of Josh Billings' lecture cards which depicts Josh seated on stage holding the head of a docile mule in his arms. The inscription "Yures without a struggle, Josh Billings" appears beside the figure, and in the upper right-hand corner the announcement, "Josh Lectures in this city to night" (15).

Besides being a curiosity, the work has little importance in the Shaw canon. It is probably the least significant of all his writings.

CHAPTER 6

Almanacs

D URING the ten-year period, 1869-79, Shaw was engaged in producing the work that was to bring him more fame than any other literary undertaking—*Josh Billings' Farmer's Allminax*, published in ten numbers by G. W. Carleton. It was an enterprise that Shaw engineered enthusiastically and profited from lucratively. In its very first year the *Allminax* sold over ninety thousand copies; the second year, one hundred and twenty-seven thousand; the third and fourth years, over one hundred thousand; and never less than fifty thousand during its remaining six years.[1] Shaw netted more than thirty thousand dollars over the decade it was published.

That the *Allminax* was so successful is not surprising, for Shaw was not only an effective writer but also an astute businessman. And as a businessman he recognized in the development of the almanac in America a chance to capitalize on its two most popular trends while producing something characteristically his own.

I *Loomings*

Shaw experimented with the idea of a humorous almanac as early as the autumn of 1867 when he published a fragmentary trial work entitled "Aulminak for 1868" in the *New York Weekly* for November 7 (reprinted in *Ice*, 234-38 as "Aulminak for 1869"). Concerned only with the first twenty days of March, this fragment is really a mere daily cataloguing of weather observations, an occasional practical aphorism ("Muny iz tight, so are briks"), satirical historical facts concerning that day (for Monday, March third—"Augustus Ceazer sighns the tempranse pledge 1286"; for Tuesday, March fourth—"Augustus Ceazer breaks the pledge 1286"), and a few hints mixed with humor to farmers concerning planting. It is obvious from this piece that Shaw did not have his future project firmly in mind; and, though there are some traces of the comic and farmer's almanacs, it is evident that Shaw was mainly feeling his way. Some excerpts exemplify:

MARCH begins on Saturday, and hangs on for 31 days.

Saturday, 1st.—Sum wind; look out for squalls, and pack peddlers; munny iz tight, so are briks. Ben Jonson had his boots tapped 1574; eggs a dollar a piece, hens on a strike; mercury 45 degrees above zero; snow, mixed with wind.

Sunday, 2nd.—Horace Greeley preaches in Grace church; text, "the gentleman in black," wind northwest, with simptoms of dust; hen strike continues; the ringleaders are finally arrested and sent to pot; eggs eazier. . . .

Sunday, 9th.—This is the Sabbath, a day that our fathers thought a good deal ov. Mutch wind (in sum ov the churches); streets lively, bissiness good; prize fight on the palisades; police reach the ground after the fight is aul over, and arrest the ropes and the ring. Wind sutherly; a lager-beer spring discovered just out ov the limits ov the city; millions are flocking out to see it.

Monday, 10th.—A gale, mile stuns are torn up bi the rutes; fight for 700 dollars and the belt, at Red Bank, Nu Jersey, between two well known roosters; oysters fust eaten on the half shell 1342, by Don Bivalvo, an Irish Duke; sun sets in the west.

Tuesday, 11th.—Roosters still fighting; indications ov wind; counterfeit Tens in circulashun on the Faro Bank; look out for them; milk only 15 cents a quart; thank the Lord, "the good time," has finally come; Don Quixot fights his first wind mill, 1510, at short range, and got whipped the second round; time 14 minnits.

9:30 P. M.—Torch-lite procession at Red Bank, in honor ov the winning rooster.

Wednesday, 12th.—Sum wind, with wet showers; showers smell strong ov dandylions and grass; gold 132 17-16; exchange on Brooklin and Williamsburgh, one cent (by the ferry boats.)

Thursday, 13th.—Bad day for the alminak bissiness; no nuze, no wind; no cards; no nothing. . . .

Monday, 17th.—Plant sum beans; plant them deep; if yu don't they will be sure tew cum up. Robinson Cruso born 1515, all alone, on a destitute iland. Warm rain, mixt with wind; woodchucks cum out ov their holes and begin tew chuck a little. . . .

Thursday, 20th.—Appearance ov rain; plant corn for early whiskey; frogs hold their fust concert—Ole Bullfrog musical direcktor—matinee every afternoon; snakes are caught wriggling (an old trick ov theirs); a warm and muggy night; yu can hear the bullheads bark; United States buys the iland ov Great Brittain. (*Ice,* 234-38)

II   Comics and Farmers

Shaw's *Josh Billings' Farmer's Allminax* was not conceived until some two years later; and, when it emerged, it was a mature progeny nurtured in the image of the almanac tradition in America, especially two of its dominant types. In many ways the entire history of the almanac[2] had its influence on Shaw's undertaking: the moralistic overtones,[3] as seen in Franklin's *Poor Richard's Almanac;* the astrological and scientific concerns, such as the Man of the Signs (*Homo Signorum*),[4] prognostications, and weather charts that appeared throughout eighteenth- and nineteenth-century almanacs; the informative aspect of almanacs that carried miscellaneous data of general interest to the reader; and the literary entertainment that dotted almanac pages in the form of poems, epigrams, jingles, conundrums, and sketches. Even the proliferation of special types of almanacs, a nineteenth-century phenomenon,[5] was important to Shaw's enterprise. Two of these types in particular afforded direct influence—the comic almanac and the farmer's. Indeed, had these two kinds not developed, Shaw would probably never have produced his almanac. His work embodied many of the techniques of the former and originated as a burlesque of the latter.

The comic almanac in America, which, as Constance Rourke has said, shows more than any other source "the wide diffusion of a native comic lore,"[6] got its start much earlier than expected. Its origin, ironically, was in the serious almanac. If authors themselves did not bring in humorous elements, as did Franklin in *Poor Richard's Almanac* beginning in 1733 and the two Nathaniel Ameses in their almanacs from 1726 to 1775, the publishers occasionally inserted bits of humor—frequently against the author's will or knowledge—between items of fact and information.[7]

The full-fledged comic almanac, however, was not inaugurated until the nineteenth century with the publication of *The Ameri-*

can Comic Almanac, which was published in Boston by Charles Ellms from 1831 until 1846. The major period of the comic almanac was, as Rourke and Charles L. Nichols confirm, between 1830 and 1860.[8] Nichols points out that more than thirty varieties of comic almanacs came out of Massachusetts alone during this period.[9] Early imitations were numerous, the most famous being the many Crockett Almanacs, the first of which was published by S. N. Dickinson in 1833 and was followed shortly by a number of rival editions spanning the years 1835 to 1856. Other popular titles of the day were *The Comic Token, Broad Grins, Finn's Comic Almanac, Yankee Doodle Comic Almanac, Uncle Sam's Almanac, Sam Slick's All-My-Neck,* and *The Devil's Comic Texas Oldmanick.*[10]

In appearance and contents most of the comic almanacs were similar, and Shaw modeled his to some extent on their formats. In size they were about 20 x 12 cm, of about thirty-six unnumbered pages, and were enclosed in illustrated covers, the front cover also serving as the title page.[11] The contents mainly consisted of jokes, humorous tales and poems, and crude illustrations.[12] The illustrations, as William Murrell has observed, were many times more humorous than the jokes and stories.[13] This comic-almanac tradition that influenced Henry Wheeler Shaw attained renewed popularity in the 1870's, 1880's, and 1890's, thus enhancing the popularity of Shaw's contribution.

The tradition of the farmer's almanac in America is as lengthy and rich as that of the comic one. Adopting titles on grounds of containing information and advice on agricultural subjects, these annuals got their start with Nathaniel Whittemore of Lexington, Massachusetts, who first published *The Farmer's Almanac* in 1713. Other popular farmer's almanacs of the eighteenth and nineteenth centuries were those by Thomas Spofford, Truman Abel, Daniel Robinson, Thomas Green Fessenden, John Smith, A. Maynard, Dudley and William B. Leavett, and one simply by Allen & Company.[14] By far the best and most famous, however, and the one that was the direct cause of *Josh Billings' Farmer's Allminax* was Robert Bailey Thomas' *(Old) Farmer's Almanac,* first printed for the year 1793 and still active. Thomas himself was proprietor for fifty-four years until his death in 1846. It then passed into the hands of nephews who kept it in the family until 1904 when its importance took a sharp decline.[15]

Thomas' immensely popular annual, appealing primarily to a rural audience, was a small 21 x 13 cm pamphlet bound in paper covers with illustrations and advertisements. Twelve of its forty-eight pages were devoted to the yearly calendar, and the main part of each calendar page was a two-column table containing astronomical calculations and weather predictions on the left and the "Farmer's Calendar" of hints and suggestions about farm routines on the right. The other thirty-six pages contained such matters as tables of American presidents; eclipses and astronomical charts; lists of colleges and county commissioners meetings in New England; information on courts (from the Supreme Court to police courts in Massachusetts); sections of literary interest with poetry, anecdotes, moral tags, and conundrums; and miscellaneous bits about birds and insects, game laws, tide tables, and post-office regulations. Also included for variety and entertainment were humorous character sketches bearing colorful and characteristic names. Such personalities as Neighbor Oldfield, Neighbor Warmshins, Captain Red Eye, Old Aunt Betty Beeswax, Tom Testy, Sam Soggy, and Tim Twilight provided much entertainment with their Yankee dialects and unpredictable deeds.[16] Two obvious omissions from Thomas' almanac, however, were the Man of the Signs and astrological predictions —features available in practically every other almanac. Thomas, who held no belief in the false science of the stars, refused to compromise on that point despite the popularity of astrology with readers.

III   Josh Enters the Scene

The highly successful *Allminax* was begun, ironically, during an illness. Shaw was on a lecture tour in March, 1869; and, while stopped in Skohegan, Maine, he was stricken by a severe cold and forced to quit his tour. Confined to bed,[17] he turned to Thomas' almanac for amusement and decided that a burlesque of this staid New England pillar was in order. Beginning his rough draft immediately, he had a manuscript for the year 1870 ready within two weeks; and, when well, he approached his publisher, G. W. Carleton, who needed no convincing. Carleton, who had already thought of the idea of a burlesque almanac, had previously but unsuccessfully approached Charles Farrar Brown, Robert H. Newell, and M. N. Thomson about such a project.

Somewhat naïvely, Shaw wanted to sell outright the first year's almanac for two hundred and fifty dollars and to furnish one for nine consecutive years for the same stipend. Carleton, however, in a most considerate move, convinced him to accept a royalty of three cents on each copy sold, an agreement which netted Shaw over thirty thousand dollars for the ten-year period instead of what would have been only twenty-five hundred dollars. Though only two thousand copies were originally published in October, 1869, and two months passed before they sold, the book suddenly caught on; and, before the next three months were over, reportedly ninety thousand copies had been bought by enthusiastic readers.[18]

Besides the three-cent royalty that Shaw collected on each twenty-five-cent copy sold, he also received remuneration from the dedication, which he decided to make serious and to secure an underwriter for, rather than use a burlesque dedication and receive no money. His first dedicatory sponsors were his employers on the *New York Weekly*, Street and Smith. In exchange for the dedication-advertisement appearing on the back side of the cover, Street and Smith paid Shaw two cents per copy the first year and one cent the second before canceling their deal out of fear, as Smith himself phrased it, "that the mysterious little book might sell a million." Thereafter, Shaw usually dedicated the almanac to some business establishment for a flat fee of five hundred dollars.[19]

IV *Burlesque Elements*

In the *Allminax,* Shaw displayed his flair for humor and satire that followed the traditions of the comic and farmer's almanacs. Seemingly, he was unaware of a few isolated cases of direct spoofing of the almanac such as Thomas Dekker's making light of the Man-of-the-Signs diagram in *The Ravens Almanacke* (1609) and in America *Poor Robin's Almanack* for 1690 that burlesqued the horoscope.[20] Shaw's attack being his own, the approach is fresh; the humor and satire are characteristically pointed but not painfully sharp. After all, he wanted to amuse devotees of the almanac and perhaps cause them to take a second look at their devotion; he did not want to alienate them.

Shaw burlesques all of the popular contents of farmer's almanacs: the Man of the Signs, monthly astronomical predictions and horoscopes, the farmer's calendar, weather predictions, supplementary stellar data such as dates of eclipses, and miscellaneous information such as civil laws, hints to farmers, and various agency regulations.

Of the Man of the Signs, Shaw was as suspicious as was R. B. Thomas; and this emblem is the butt of much ridicule in the *Allminax*. A chart of the *Homo Signorum* (a human figure surrounded by signs of the Zodiac which influence various parts of the body) with an explanation of the chart stands as the first page in each of the ten issues. Shaw introduced some ingenious comic alterations, however, of what is customary on such charts. On the one for 1870 above the *Homo Signorum* Shaw writes, "The undersighned iz an Amerikan brave, in hiz grate tragick akt ov being attaked bi the twelve constellashuns.—(*May the best man win.*)" Then, after the conventional chart, he facetiously gives a key "Tew the Abov Performance," emphasizing the nonsense of astrological interpretations: "Tew kno exackly whare the sighn iz, multiply the day ov the month bi the sighn, then find a dividend that will go into a divider four times without enny remains, subtrackt this from the sighn, add the fust quoshunt tew the last divider, then multiply the whole ov the man's boddy bi all the sighns, and the result will be jist what yu are looking after."

On the chart for 1871, Shaw substitutes his own slate of animals and insects for the traditional figures of the constellations and, further to satirize the pedantic terminology of astrology, assigns each creature a spurious Latin name:

(*Stinggus,*) the Hornet.	(*Saltuss,*) the Kodfish.
(*Bugguss,*) a Cockroach.	(*Buzzuss,*) a Fly.
(*Roottus,*) the Swine.	(*Struttus,*) the Ruseter.
(*Crawluss,*) a Angleworm.	(*Munkuis,*) a Munkee.
(*Buttuss,*) the Gote.	(*Stealuss,*) the Coon.
(*Sneakuss,*) a Kat.	(*Foxus,*) a Fox.

The year 1872 being leap year, Shaw explains that "the sighns of the Zodiak are all on the rampage," and he shows in that chart the Gemini twins playing leapfrog; Taurus, Aries, and the other animals are frolicking; Sagittarius sportingly shoots his bow; Aquarius (a funny little man with a watering can) is avidly sprinkling his garden. All are on a jubilant spree. The next year Shaw jests with the idea of local versus universal limitations of stellar prognoses by stating under the signs, "The above zodiak sighns are kalkulated expressly for the meridian ov Pordunk, Pa., [the signs have all been transformed into countryfied figures] but will answer for Nu Orleans, Nova Skoshia, or Greenland's icy mountains." In the 1874 chart the Man, surrounded by a strange conglomeration of signs, is reading a copy of the *New York Weekly*, while the inscription for the chart of 1877 jokingly quips:

Stranger! wouldst thou kno whar the sighn iz?
Lo, and behold! "thou paze thy munny, and thou takest thine choice."

After such appearances as these in the *Allminax*, the Man of the Signs is left without much dignity, and Shaw has made his point.

The signs of the zodiac themselves lose their dignity throughout the *Allminax*. The heading of each calendar page for the year 1879 contains an etching of one of the twelve signs and then, immediately under the etching, offers a comic explanation of the sign: for Pisces, "Two Perch—possibly one Smelt"; Aries, "On the War Path.—The hit ov the seazon"; Taurus, "Bound for Wall Street.—Bring on Yure Bear"; Cancer, "A Shell-Fish—pretty much all shell"; Leo, "Strayed or Stolen.—Return to P. T. Barnum"; Virgo, "Sweet 16 (*sub rosa* 38)"; Scorpio, "When the pinch comes, he is thar." Furthermore, the signs are the subjects of humorous monographs appearing opposite the calendar pages of the *Allminax* for 1873. A characteristic example of their cleverness is the one on Aquarius:

AQUARIUS, THE ZODIAK WATERMAN.

Aquarius duz the sprinkling pot bizzness for the zodiak. He kan be seen enny klear day up in the zodiak laying the dust which the other zodiakers kik up. He iz a quiet old gent about 5 foot 6, and wears a wool hat, and a bull's eye watch. Who hiz ansestors waz no one kan tell. He iz an old bachelor now, but they tell me, up in the zodiak, that he alwus takes the most pains when he sprinkles in front ov Virgo. Thare iz a tradishun in Pordunk, that Aquarius was once a tempranse lekturer, but gitting too thin for the bizzness waz translated, and sot to sprinkling in the zodiak. Aquarius haz charge ov the leggs amung the sighns in the zodiak, and i notis that water iz better for the legs than sum other fluids i know.

The *Allminax* offers much burlesque of astrological lore beyond the *Homo Signorum* and zodiac. Typical of the calendar pages in farmer's almanacs was the column of prognostications appearing to the left of the "Farmer's Calendar" column. With a note and astrological sign by each day in the month, this column offered weather and tide predictions; data on sun, moon, and constellar positions; and important events in history corresponding with that day. Shaw's burlesque of this column includes embellishing the signs and rearranging them nonsensically or making humorous designs with them (like a human face), including trivial information ("The fust flea kaught" on this day, or "lemonade diskovered 1306"), and giving weather predictions of dubious value ("the kold iz kold" on this day).[21]

The 1872 issue contains burlesque horoscopes for each month which point up the absurdity of predicting the patterns of life for persons born in a particular month. The horoscopes for June —one for males, the other females—are as follows:

The male individual born during June will be one of 7 children, but not the only one. He will hav 3 brothers, and one sister, who will marry a hard shell baptist preacher. He will studdy law, and enter the profeshun with gilt edge prospekts, but his fust klient being a counterfiter, whom he succeeds in gitting clear, and receiving 50 dollars in counterfit money for his services, disgusts him with the bizzness.

The female who appears on the platform this month will alwus hav cause tew wonder whi she did it. Her father will be a skool teacher, and he will bring her up in the distrikt skool bizzness. At 29 years and six months she will marry, and will be well edukated in the dutys ov a wife, for she will understand Daball's arithmetik, and parseing, just az eazy az falling down the cellar stairs. She will hav but one son, and he will be edukated oph from hiz feet at an early age.

Satiric monographs on the months appear in 1870, and Shaw spoofs the origins and the characteristics of each month, as in the one for July:

July iz the sixth month, which ackounts for its being so near the middle ov the year. It derives its name from "Julos" a hot old phellow, who settled near the equator, at an early day, and kept every boddy in hiz naborhood, in a profound swett. July haz menny features ov *interest*, the *principle* one ov which, iz, the payment ov semiannual *interest*, by most ov the banks, on the fust day ov the month, upon their *principal*. This iz a fine old custom, and i hope it will be kept up, for i own a leetle bank stock, and take sum *interest* in the *principle*.

Other satiric astrological elements appear at random through-out the issues. A table of "extra eklipses" appears in 1870 with such notes as "Thare will be semiockasional eklipses ov the moon, kauzed bi brandy smashes gitting between that virtewous and pale old woman, and the eyes ov sum ov our most promising young men." A list of "Kalkulashuns ov a Prognostix Natur" in 1871 ridicules the penchant for interpreting signs; for example, "Whenever yu see a flok ov geese all standing on one leg, except the old gander, and he chawing hiz cud, look out for a south-west wind tewmorrow, or the next day, or the day after, or at sum fewter time." New England weather watchers are the target in a mock weather synopsis appearing in 1873: "The byrometer will rize very sudden this morning at Pordunk, 3 foot, and fall the like amount at Sakramento City. The diffikulty in the weather for the last 2 days, which haz predominated at Boston and around New Orleans, waz owing tew the byrometer at Pordunk being took down and sent tew the blacksmiths shop for repairs."

Of course farmer's almanacs, as has been shown with R. B. Thomas', contained far more than astrological information; and Shaw also burlesqued these contents. Since rules and regulations of various sorts were printed in almanacs, Shaw's 1871 issue carries a list of "Rules, By-Laws, and Regulations" for the "Por-dunk Valley Rail Road." In such burlesque rules as "Conduktors are positively forbid trieing tew pass each other on a single track" Shaw attacks the frequent irrelevance and foolishness of official regulations. Much the same spirit is found in his slate of "Konnektikut Blew Laws" in the 1871 *Allminax*: "No man must chu enny tobbacko on the sabbath day unless he goes down cellar and duz it."

There are also the numerous hints to farmers scattered throughout the *Allminax*. Shaw's are humorous and satiric. The best way to find the square root of a hog's nose, he advises the farmer, is to turn him into a garden patch. The farmer should keep a cow so that the milk will have to be watered only once. To make a hoe cake, boil a hoe until it jells and then let it cake. To break a mule, "commence at his head." Concerning crops, "Turnips should be planted near the top ov the ground, if yu want them tew turn up good," and "Egg plants iz good, but eggs sot under a stiddy hen will produce more chickens than they will tew plant them."

V   *Standard Fare*

Although basically satiric, the *Allminax* contains much that is simply the usual humorous material found in Shaw's works. As Jeannette Tandy has observed, "The forms which he had already developed, Yankee aphorisms, mock advertisements, advice to correspondents, moral essays on the vegetables, beasts, and men were peculiarly adapted to this venture."[22] Headings of calendar pages, for instance, carry humorous verses and conundrums much like those in *Josh Billings' Spice Box*. The farmer's calendar column itself, which R. B. Thomas used for hints on crop planting and maintenance of equipment, Shaw transforms into a column of humorous asphorisms like those appearing in his other works.

Short comic monographs appear on pages opposite the calendar pages; and the subjects—when not directly almanac elements—range from catalogues of animals and insects to the Billings family tree. In most issues of the *Allminax* these monologues are a related series, but occasionally—and especially toward the end of the venture—they are a miscellaneous hodgepodge. In addition, there is humorous advertising, much of it "plugging" issues of the *Allminax*. On one of these pages, entitled "How They Do Talk About *Josh Billings' Farmer's Allminax*," Shaw gives comments by readers (statements actually of his own invention) lauding the enterprise. "Giv me liberty, or giv me deth, but if i kant hav either, giv me Josh Billings' allminax for 1870," cries one enthusiastic reader. Another blurb attests, "It kured mi wife ov wanting to die." To round out the humorous complexion of the *Allminax*, Shaw included comic illustrations by Livingston Hopkins and also amusing miscellaneous filler items.

Shaw's own advertising of the *Allminax*, incidentally, spread beyond the pages of the booklet itself into the pages of the *New York Weekly*. The following letter to the editors of the *Weekly* appeared on November 10, 1870; and it is only one example of a blurb written by Shaw for his own work:

Editors New York Weekly:

Sum men are born grate, sum git grate after they are born, sum have grateness hove upon them, and sum aint troubled with neither.

But (my dear phello) the objekt in writing this epistol iz not this, but to inform you that I shall let loose about the middle ov Oktober, 1870, "JOSH BILLINGS FARMERS ALLMANAX FOR 1871."

No family who keeps a two hoss carriage should be without this Allmanax.

Az anshunt Knower, phull of phaith, let slip the pure and innocent duv from his Ark, so doth i let slip this Allmanax, and hope it wont come back. All good housewifes will find in this Allmanax, how to train up their husbands in the way they should go, and they wont depart from it, and also how to make a lively slap jax.

To the weary wanderer this Allmanax will be a gide board, showing the nearest cut to the next town, and to the sorry, a soda fountain ov gimnastic delight.

This Allmanax gives the biography, etimology, syntax, and prosidy ov bugs, beasts, and little cod fishes, and tells us, with the fondness ov a step parent, the right time to trade oph a dog.

In konklushun, it gives me grate plezzure tew remark,

That kussid are lobsters and milk for supper, for they hav no bowells ov mercy, nor mercy for bowells.

With grate flexibility of karacter, I am your limber friend.

JOSH BILLINGS,
Allminacter. (p. 4)

Thus, there was enough general humorous material in the ten issues of the *Allminax* to prevent it from being solely a burlesque of the farmer's almanac. Audiences could also enjoy it as a jest book.

VI *Popularity and Demise*

Shaw's original ten-year contract terminated in 1879, and he chose to quit "allminaxing" probably because of his heavy work as lecturer and columnist and also undoubtedly somewhat from ennui. The *Allminax*, nevertheless, was his favorite undertaking; and his most treasured book was the one-volume edition of the ten issues published by Carleton in 1879 under the title *Old Probability: Perhaps Rain—Perhaps Not*, the book he referred to affectionately as "My Little Waif."[23]

The popularity and financial rewards of the *Allminax* also indicate its favoritism with thousands of readers. When the *Hamilton Literary Monthly* reviewer praised it, he singled out Shaw's aphorisms which "often rival in wisdom those of 'Poor Richard' himself; while they are exquisitely cool and humorous."[24] Street and Smith lauded it perennially in the *New York Weekly*, their hyperboles echoing in part, of course, their own vested interest in Shaw's success. Their advertisement for the 1874 issue proclaimed that the *Allminax* for 1874 "is about the richest and raciest little work that has ever been published."[25] And for 1875 they raved, "The enormous advance demand for this famous comic almanac, and the immense sale all over the country, render its appearance one of the events of the publishing year."[26]

Mark Twain's praiseful comment that the *Allminax* "is a pleasant conceit and happily executed"[27] seems best to clinch the strength and appeal of the work. Whether or not modern readers peruse almanacs or newspaper horoscopes, they can still delight in Shaw's abundant burlesque of astrology. The monographs are witty and pleasant to read; the humorous aphorisms are among Shaw's most poignant. It is a work that simultaneously entertains the modern reader and causes him to ponder the interests and customs of an older, rural America that relied heavily on monthlies and annuals for entertainment and information.

CHAPTER 7

Josh on the Platform

WHEN Shaw took to the platform in the middle 1860's and became a nationally known comic lecturer, he joined one of the richest traditions in nineteenth-century American culture. The lecture system was widespread and highly popular during the century, appealing in its serious vein to audiences on instructional and moralistic grounds, in its humorous bent to their need for entertainment. Organized lecturing had its "official" start in 1826 when Josiah Holbrook founded the first local lyceum,[1] and by 1831 the American Lyceum, a national organization, was established. Though lyceums involved various types of programs, lecturing soon became their dominant forte because of the appeal of eminent speakers—such as Ralph Waldo Emerson, E. P. Whipple, Theodore Parker, and Henry Ward Beecher—and because of the educational value of such programs. By 1850 lecture halls were as essential public facilities in the West as in the East. And also, shortly after that date, the boards began to ring with new tones to rival the old as the funny men—Billings, Ward, Nasby, and Twain—undertook to display their comic wares in person.

I *A Rugged Beginning*

In Shaw's young, single days, when he was in his twenties, he had enjoyed two amateurish successes on the platform: one as Mordacai David in Indiana and the other as himself lecturing on "Milk" in Norwalk, Ohio (see Chapter 1). In 1863, now forty-five and with an established reputation in Poughkeepsie as a humorist because of his early newspaper writings, he was approached by two of the town's leading citizens—the Reverend Leonard Corning and the Honorable George W. Sterling—and asked to deliver a comic lecture as part of a night of local entertainment they were planning. Hesitant at first, Shaw at last consented, prepared his lecture, and read it for practice to the two gentlemen who were, as Cyril Clemens relates, "agreeably surprised and delighted at the marvelous talent the neophyte had of combining wisdom, humor, and shrewd observation, all in one sentence."[2] The lecture was so successful with the public that his friends scheduled him for more—still on the local front—and Shaw began to feel quite confident about "Putty and Varnish," the catchall title he gave to his rather discursive talk.

Nothing but years of dismal failure, however, followed his initial triumphs. Encouraged by the receptiveness of his home townsmen, Shaw let an enthusiastic former printer from western New York, who had been impressed with "Putty and Varnish," talk him into being his manager for a lecture tour West (as far as Milwaukee). The trip was a mistake. In a cavernous hall in one town, there was only one person in the audience; Shaw invited him out to eat. In another city twenty were there; Shaw refunded their money. At the end of the season, Shaw and his manager barely had enough funds to return to Poughkeepsie.[3]

The next year, 1864, however, found Shaw returning doggedly to the platform, having worked diligently on his program and having been urged on by friends. Again he was a failure, and he returned once more to Poughkeepsie, convinced this time that he had delivered his last lecture; for it appeared that he simply did not have a big enough name outside his local area to attract attention to his offerings. But a year later he unexpectedly received a telegram from the Norwich, Connecticut, YMCA reading "What will you charge, and when can you deliver a lecture for us? Answer."[4] Shaw was surprised, to say the least, since a year before he had spoken in Norwich and, in his opinion, unsuccessfully so. However, he was encouraged enough to gamble one more time, and he made the trip. On lecture night in Norwich, every seat in the hall was occupied, an unexplainable phenomenon (except that Shaw must have been more successful there the preceding year than he had thought). Response to his lecture—a performance now greatly revised and polished—was electric.

As a result, Shaw suddenly found himself in constant

demand as a lecturer. Within three years of this successful night, his platform career was assured when he received an offer from James Clark Redpath, manager of the famous Boston Lyceum, to come under the sponsorship of his bureau. Redpath, erstwhile journalist and publisher, and his associate George L. Fall were establishing the Redpath (or Boston) Lyceum Bureau in 1869; and, in so doing, were soon to give a major boost to a diffuse but somewhat dying vogue. The American Lyceum had been dissolved in 1839 when other organizations such as boards of education arose to assume its educational functions, and the lecture system had become mainly a local, and thus highly disorganized, affair by mid-century. Since there was no longer a central clearing house, lecturers and managers bore the full brunt of arranging engagements, and cities—especially the small ones—often had to take whomever they could get and count themselves fortunate to get anyone. By the eve of Redpath's entrance into the business, thus, the system was chaotic.

Redpath's Bureau, according to J. B. Pond, prominent New York lecture manager, caused lectures in the latter half of the century to increase tenfold over what they were in 1860.[5] The Bureau was a central handling agency that arranged for the circuits through all states and communities in the northern United States and Canada that wanted to be included. All that local lyceums had to do was contact Redpath, and their towns would join the list of communities in line to hear such men as Billings, Nasby, Twain, Beecher, Greeley, and Wendell Phillips. All participating local lyceums, of course, wanted the big names. Redpath's agreement assured them of these celebrities but also required them to engage several unknowns afterward—"house-emptiers" as well as "house-fillers," as Mark Twain termed them.[6]

Advantages for the lecturers, both famous and unknown, were many. Redpath offered attractive fees of at least one hundred dollars a night for celebrities like Billings; twenty-five to fifty dollars for lesser knowns.[7] Redpath's commission was 10 percent, but he relieved the lecturers of the responsibility of making their own arrangements, of setting them up for anywhere from eighty to two hundred guaranteed engagements (depending

upon their popularity) during the season (which generally ran
from October to March), and of handling all the liaison work
with local committees through his Bureau.

E. P. Hingston, Artemus Ward's lecture manager, described
the convenience to the lecturer: "The lecturer experiences very
little trouble except that inseparable from travel. All his arrangements are made by the society's agent. When he arrives at where
he is to lecture, there is sure to be a committee-man waiting to
receive him, and when he has finished his lecture and received
his fee, he will be either escorted to his hotel by some of the
chief members of the Lyceum, or invited to sup and sleep at a
private home, where he will be regarded as a lion and treated
more as a member of the family than as a stranger."[8]

Finally, Lyceum headquarters in School Street, Boston, offered
the lecturers a congenial home ground and meeting place when
they were in that area. Here frequently Billings, Twain, and
Nasby met and held gab fests or went off together in search of
entertainment.[9] The lecturers, according to Paine, "put up at
Young's Hotel, and spent their days at the bureau, smoking and
spinning yarns, or talking shop. Early in the evening they scattered to the outlying towns, Lowell, Lexington, Concord, New
Bedford."[10]

The advantages of the Bureau, thus, were so numerous that
Shaw naturally accepted Redpath's invitation; and for fifteen
consecutive seasons Josh Billings read his lectures with rousing
success, thereby becoming a privileged one-hundred-dollar-a-
night-man and reading his lectures from fifty to one hundred
nights a year in, as F. S. Smith colorfully observed, "every town
on this continent that has twenty thousand people in it, and in
hundreds of towns that have not got a thousand in them."[11] As
Shaw himself said, he had appeared "in every town in Texas
and California and in all the Canada towns and then down
South from Baltimore across to Memphis and into New Orleans."[12] In his lecturing as in his writing, Shaw found that he
had "struck oil."

II *Josh on Stage: Subjects and Techniques*

Shaw's repertoire consisted of a few basic lectures, one of
which was usually selected for the duration of an individual,

entire tour. Communications were so poor in his day that there was little chance that the audiences in the next town would learn what had been said in a neighboring community the preceding evening. His initial lecture, "Putty and Varnish," was used all along the circuit during the first years of his career. He also had talks on "Natral History," which he used in 1869-70, and on "Specimen Bricks," delivered on an 1874 western tour. Another, the title capitalizing on his almanac fame—"The Probability of Life, Perhaps Rain, Perhaps not"—was delivered for one hundred nights in 1880 from Eastport, Maine, to Pittsburgh, Pennsylvania.[13] The "Pensive Cockroach," a natural-history talk, was still another title.[14]

But the three lectures which became his mainstays throughout his years on the platform were "Buty and the Beasts," "What i Kno about Hotels," and especially "Milk." They are the ones Shaw referred to jokingly as being "all that i own, and are enuff tew ruin enny man who haz got a faint heart and poor digestion."[15] "I hav red them," he wrote to the *New York Weekly*, "over 5 hundred times, to all sized aujiences, from less than 30 souls (one-half ov theze ded-heds) to three thousand seated, and 250 standing up" (October 13, 1873, 4).

Each of his lectures was a loosely constructed talk covering a multitude of subjects. The titles were either suggestive of one of the subjects in the lecture, or they sometimes had no bearing at all on the subject matter. The one entitled "What i Kno about Hotels," in addition to its paragraphs concerning hotels, included vignettes on farming, the dandy, whistling, the busy body, contentment, the district schoolmaster, the dog, and the ant.[16] "Buty and the Beasts," in which Shaw explains he takes the part of the beauty, covers some eighteen subjects, from cockroaches to angleworms, to kissing, to tight boots.[17] Shaw periodically changed the contents of a lecture while retaining the same title. One version of the famous "Milk" (which had nothing to do with milk) treated Long Branch, human happiness, the live man, the handsome man, the passionate man, the shade tree, the fastidious person, patience, the domestic man, the jealous man, and rats.[18] Another version dealt with comic lecturing, Long Branch, the rooster, the mule, the bumblebee, the hornet, flirts, the dandy, marriage, courting, advice to lecture committees, the schoolmaster, and "twelve square remarks."[19] Thus, there was frequent overlapping of subjects from lecture to lecture.

Each subject in the lecture was presented in a few short paragraphs which were often aphoristic. Shaw continued, then, to use the pithy, abrupt utterances even on the stage. The aphorism was well adapted to his lectures: succinct, it provided short, witty gems which were easy for the audience to grasp and react to quickly and appreciatively.

There was frequently little pretense in a Shaw lecture of smooth or logical transitions. The last line of one subject might read, "In delivering a comik lektur it iz a good general rule to stop sudden, sometime before yu git through." Then would follow unexpectedly, "This brings me to Long Branch."[20] Occasionally Shaw even jested about the matter of transitions. In an essay delineating the many subjects of his lecture "Buty and the Beasts," he explains that, when delivering the talk, he moves from the pedestrian topic of roosters to that of kissing, with "the most natral and eazy transishun ever attempted bi enny orator who haz trod the didaktrik boards at this point . . . ,"[21] as if there could be such a bridge. At other times one subject led somewhat logically into the next, such as, "The man or mule who can't do any hurt in this world kan't do any good . . . . This brings me to the Mule—the pashunt Mule."[22]

Shaw's personal appearance and mannerisms, as well as his carefully studied stage techniques, added to the comic tone of the evening's program. Tall and stoop-shouldered, he had a large head and massive face appointed with unusually long hair (grown to conceal an unsightly birthmark on his neck), a shaggy beard, and deep-set, thoughtful eyes.[23] He wore a solemn black suit and boots, shirts with oversized collars, and no necktie. When this half-dignified, half-comical looking oddity appeared unannounced on the platform (he avoided the customary introduction by a member of the local lecture committee) and then sat to lecture (he rarely stood), the evening's gaiety had begun. The table he sat behind contained a podium and, when the subject was "Milk," a pitcher and glass of milk which were usually unexplained and completely ignored.[24] Studying his audience for a moment, usually with deadpan expression, he then began speaking his lines from a prepared text deliberately and dryly for the sixty- to ninety-minute program, making abundant use of anticlimactic and periodic sentences. "Milk" began, as quoted with interpolations by Eli Perkins:

Ladies and Gentlemen:—
I hope you are all well. [Looking over his glasses.]
Thare is lots ov folks who eat well and drink well, and yet are sick all the time. Theze are the folks who alwuz "enjoy poor health."
Then I kno lots ov people whoze only reckomendashun iz, that they are helthy——so iz an onion. [Laughter.]
The subject of my lecture is Milk—plain M-i-l-k.
The best thing I've ever seen on milk is cream. [Laughter.]
That's right [joining]. "People of good sense" are thoze whoze opinyuns agree with ours. [Laughter.]
People who agree with you never bore you. The shortest way to a woman's harte iz to praze her baby and her bonnet, and to a man's harte to praze hiz watch, hiz horse and hiz lectur.
Eliar Perkins sez a man iz a bore when he talks so much about hisself that you kant talk about yourself. [Laughter.]
Still I shall go on talking.[25]

Going beyond the humor of the subjects themselves, Shaw resorted to stunts such as halting in the midst of his delivery, peering over his glasses at a restless young man in the audience, and remarking, to the utter delight of the audience, "Yung man, please set down, and keep still, yu will hav plenty ov chances yet to make a phool ov yureself before yu die."[26] Or he would, like Twain, lead up to a punch line or conclusion and then break off due to some trivial distraction, perhaps or perhaps not returning to the point he was about to make. He would say, "A man never gits to be a fust klass phool until he haz reached seventy years, and falls in luv with a bar maid of 19, and marries her, and then,—" and then reach for his watch, begin winding it, and say absently to the audience, "You kant do two things to wonst,"[27] a trick that rarely failed to convulse an attentive audience.

The tone of an evening with Josh Billings was often pre-established to some extent by one or more of Shaw's advertising gimmicks. He sometimes printed humorous announcements of forthcoming lectures, such as this one that appeared on a postal card in 1877:

"Josh Billings and the Young Man." Young man, don't kry for spilt milk, but pik up yure pail and milking stool, and go for the next cow. Yures affekshionately, Josh Billings. For sale or To Let. Price Neat, But Not Gaudy. Contemplating a trip to California during the winter of 1877, I will read my old and venerable lecture, "MILK," before any association who may desire to hear it. The "Milk" in this lecture is condensed, and will keep sweet in any climate.

"Your cheerful friend,

Josh Billings."[28]

Still another card read:

JOSH BILLINGS

Will Deliver his Plaintiff Discourse on

"Natral History"

(and warrant it for 60 days)

at   Hall,

On   Evening.

It is with the most grave apprehensions that I consent to read a discourse on "Natral History," a subject so nearly exhausted by the following distinguished authors. . . . Josh Billings, (521 Broadway, New York)[29]

The "distinguished authors," of course, were not listed. Another favorite stunt card of Shaw's was a combination advertisement and program card for "Milk" that had the word "over" in large type at the bottom of the card, but the back was totally blank.[30]

Finally, the *New York Weekly* helped set the comic tone for many of Shaw's appearances by occasionally carrying a record of his tours, by describing his successes, and by running advertisements that played up Josh's humor. One sizable advertisement in the *Weekly* for a lecture in the autumn of 1880, for example, carried Thomas Nast's illustrations of Josh at the podium and underneath announced, in glowing terms, the forthcoming appearances of Josh at Steinway Hall for his lecture on "Milk." The advertisement advises "the lovers of genuine humor to prepare for the great event" (October 27, 1880, 4).

III   *"An Unkommon Pesky Thing"*

The role of the comic lecturer was anything but easy, and Shaw was not so glib over his success as to be insensitive to its difficulties. The lecturer always had to worry about audience reactions: would the crowd be friendly, hostile, indifferent? Sometimes audience sentiments were mixed, a state as unsettling to the lecturer as if he faced hostility. Shaw wrote the *Weekly* from Council Bluffs, Iowa, while on his 1874 western trip: "I lektured here at the Opera house to about 600 guests who were differently affekted; sum were mad, and sum were glad, and menny ov them couldn't seem to decide what did ail them" (July 6, 1874, 4). At other times, audiences were simply indifferent: "I pronounced 'Milk' last night," Shaw wrote the *Weekly*, "to a slightly numerous lot ov spektators, i hardly know whether they love me to-day or not; they kept still, which iz one evidence ov respekt....Comic Lektring doz better, for a stiddy diet, on applauze, than it doz on profound respekt..." (February 27, 1868, 6).

Facing a particularly discriminating audience, like the one at Boston, was a special strain on comic lecturers because they had to worry about how cosmopolites would react to their informality and homespun wit. Boston was the crucial test of a lecturer's mettle; in fact, lectures were never delivered initially in Boston but were first tried in surrounding towns. When perfected, they were put to the test in Boston Music Hall; and if successful, as Paine points out, "the rest of the season was safe."[31] With unusual trepidation, Shaw wrote the *Weekly* prior to his lecture in Boston: "I am playkarded to lektur here to-night at Musik Hall, but how i shall succeed the Lord only knows, for i, a man of no learning, a very poor speller, and devoid of impudense, and got to face poets and skollars, historyans and sages, besides lots of wimmin, who hav got mo edukashun in one minnit than Nebudkenezzer had after 999 years of toil and sweat.... I shall probably make a fizzle of it, but i have one consolashun to cheer me, it won't be mi fust fizzle" (February 17, 1870, 2).[32]

There were always newspapers critics to be concerned about too. Though Shaw usually drew favorable reviews, he was occasionally panned. While on his western tour in 1874, he wrote back to the *Weekly*, with amusing understatement, "Sum ov the nuzepaper kritiks don't admire mi lekturs az much az they ought to, they say that the material iz too old." He then quipped that "theze fellows would objekt to the 10 commandments for the same reazon" (July 6, 1874, 4). In short, a lecturer never knew

what to expect from his listeners. Shaw once commented that
he always considered comic lecturing "as unsertain az the mish-
ionary bizzness"[33] and complained further:

Next tew finding the North Pole kommik lekturing iz the hardest
thing for man tew do.

The grate trouble iz, that what seems az phull ov phun, and even
wit to the lekturer, az a blown up bladder phalls on the aujience az
phlatt and klammy as a half-baked slapjack.

Yu kant tell how humor iz a going tew take, enny more than yu
kan kalkulate how kastor ile iz a gowing tew take on a wodden image.

Experience iz no use tew yu in theze matters, for i hav bin a
good while in the bizzness, and aint half so certain now ov suckcess
az i waz the fust time i opened mi throttle valve, and let steam
on to a gathring ov people in front ov me.

The more i tri tew reduse humor to a science, the more i find out
that i am a kondem phool.[34]

Certain routines on the lecture circuit added to its difficulties.
Shaw disliked having to stay in seclusion until lecture time; he
wanted to mingle with the people of a new community and learn
more about his favorite subject—humanity. But seclusion was a
necessity, as he explains:

It dont do, tew go around among the grocerys, telling who yu
are, and eating hard biled eggs and popped korn, folks will git
yure heft, and aint apt tew lay it too high, each one makes up hiz
mind, and the most ov them cum tew the konklusion, that you aint
mutch of a kuss after all.

We hav tew stay hid in our rooms, and be seen for the fust time
in front ov the audience, led out with a halter on, az you would
lead out a babboon.

Thus we start even with the audience, who haven't had a chance
tew buck agin the impreshion that eating hard biled eggs and
strutting around town iz apt tew inspire. (*Weekly*, February 6,
1868, 3)

Many such customs of the lecture circuit slightly irritated,
but also amused, Shaw. Among them were the stereotyped mannerisms of local lecture committees whose representatives were
in charge of greeting the lecturer upon his arrival and overseeing

his visit. With tongue in cheek, Shaw spelled out some corrective advice to such lecture committees:

1. Don't hire enny man tew lektur for yu (never mind how moral he iz) unless yu kan make munny on him.

2. Selekt 10 ov yure best looking and most talking members tew meet the lekturer at the depot.

3. Don't fail tew tell the lekturer at least 14 times on yure way from the depot tew the hotel that yu hav got the smartest town in kreashun, and sevral men in it that are wuth over a millyun.

4. When yu reach the hotel introduce the lekturer immejiately to at least 25 ov yure fust klass citizens, if yu hav tew send out for them.

5. When the lekturer's room iz reddy go with him in masse to hiz room and remind him 4 or 5 more times that yu had over 3 thousand people in yure city at the last censuss, and are a talking about having an opera house.

6. Don't leave the lekturer alone in his room over 15 minnits at once; he might take a drink out ov his flask on the sli if yu did.

7. When yu introjuce the lekturer tew the aujience don't fail tew make a speech ten or twelve feet long, occupying a haff an hour, and if you kan ring in sumthing about the growth ov yure butiful sitty, so mutch the better.

8. Always seat 9 or 10 ov the kommitty on the stage, and then if it iz a kommik lektur, and the kommitty don't laff a good deal, the aujence will konklude that the lektur iz a failure; and if they do laff a good deal, the aujence will konklude they are stool-pigeons.

9. Jist az soon az the lectur iz thru bring 75 or 80 ov the richest ov yure populashun up onto the stage and let them squeeze the hand and exchange talk with the lekturer.

10. Go with the lekturer from the hall tew hiz room in a bunch, and remind him once or twice more on the way that yure sitty iz a growing very rapidly, and ask him if he don't think so.

11. If the lekturer should inquire how the comik lekturers had succeeded who had preceded him, don't forget tew tell him that they were all failures. This will enable him tew guess what they will say about him just az soon az he gits out ov town.

12. If the lekturer's fee should be a hundred dollars or more, don't hesitate tew pay him next morning, about 5 minnits before the train leaves, in old, lop-eared one-dollar bills, with a liberal sandwitching ov tobbakko-stained shinplasters.

13. I forgot tew say that the fust thing yu should tell a lekturer, after yu had sufficiently informed him ov the immense growth ov

yure citty, iz that yure people are not edukated up tew lekturs yet, but are grate on nigger-minstrels.

14. If it iz konvenient, i would alwus hav a boy or two selling peanuts amung the aujience, during the lekture, at 5 cents a kupfull.

15. Never fail tew ask the lekturer whare he finds the most appreshiated aujiences, and he won't fail tew tell yu (if he iz an honest man) that thare ain't no state in the Union that begins tew kompare with yures.

16. Let 15 or 20 ov yure kommitty go with the lekturer, next morning, tew the kars, and az each one shakes hands with him with a kind ov deth grip, don't forget tew state that yure citty iz growing very mutch in people.

17. If the night iz wet, and the inkum ov the house won't pay expenses, don't hesitate tew make it pay by taking a chunk out ov the lekturer's fee. The lekturers all like this, but they are too modest, as a klass, tew say so.

18. I know ov several other good rules tew follow, but the abuv will do tew begin with.[35]

It is little wonder that Shaw, reflecting on its difficulties, dubbed comic lecturing "an unkommon pesky thing to do" (despite the fact that he really enjoyed it) and explained:

It iz more unsarting than the rat ketching bizzness az a means ov grace, or az a means of livelyhood.

Most enny boddy thinks they kan do it, and this iz jist what makes it so bothersum tew do.

When it iz did jist enuff, it iz a terifick success, but when it iz overdid, it iz like a burnt slapjax, very impertinent. . . .

If a lekturer trys tew be phunny, he iz like a hoss trying to trot backwards, pretty apt tew trod on himself.

Humor must fall out ov a mans mouth, like musik out ov a bobalink, or like a yung bird out ov its nest, when it iz feathered enuff to fly. . . .

The man who iz anxious tew git before an aujience, with what he calls a comik lektur, ought tew be put immediately in the stocks, so that he kant do it, for he iz a dangerous person tew git loose, and will do sum damage.

It iz a very pleazant bizzness tew make people laff, but thare iz mutch odds whether they laff *at you*, or laff at *what yu say*. . . .

Everyboddy feels az tho they had a right tew criticize a comik lectur, and most ov them do it jist az a mule criticizes things, by shutting up both eyes and letting drive with hiz two behind leggs. . . .

I dont urge enny boddy tew cultivate the comik lektring, but if they feel phull ov something, they kan't tell what, that bites, and makes them feel ridikilous, so that they kan't even saw wood without laffing tew themselfs all the time, i suppose they hav got the fun ailment in their bones, and had better let it leak out in the shape ov a lektur. . . .

If i had a boy who showed enny strong marks ov being a comik critter, if i couldn't get it out ov him enny other way, i would jine him to the Shakers, and make him weed onions for three years, just for fun.[36]

Whatever comic lecturing required of the speaker in such matters as awareness of comic timing, knowledge of audience psychology, and so forth, it demanded above all—as Shaw was quick to point out—"a man of grate strength."[37] Shaw obviously met the requirement; despite its many hardships, he always felt lecturing was "a grate deal ov phun."[38]

IV *Travel and Success*

As early as 1867, before Shaw even became associated with Redpath's Bureau, the *New York Weekly* remarked on his extensive travels on the lecture circuit: "This ubiquitous 'sum of all comicalities' does about as much 'sloshing around' as all the rest of our comic lecturers put together" (December 26, 1867, 4). The article went on to list Shaw's lecture engagements for December and January for twenty-four cities in Indiana, Wisconsin, Illinois, Iowa, and Michigan and speculated that if he were to lecture in New York City he "would crowd the Cooper institute to repletion." Shaw went to almost every section of the country—major tours canvassing the Midwest in 1868, the East (including the formidable mecca, Boston) in 1869, back to the Midwest in the early 1870's, to the Rockies and on to the West Coast in 1874. In 1882 he was even invited by a company in London to perform for a hundred nights in England, Scotland, and Ireland—an offer which he rejected for domestic reasons.[39]

Shaw never ceased to be surprised over his successes as a lecturer. There were, of course, occasional aloof or small audiences; and these naturally disappointed him. But generally reactions were highly favorable. In Galesburgh, Illinois, he found that his

"Milk" "goes down with both old and young."[40] Of midwestern audiences in general he wrote the *Weekly*: "They hav dealt most kindly with me, listening with grate politeness tew mi simple beverege, and never failing tew holler, in the right spot, louder than the 'milk' deserved" (February 6, 1868, 3). Referring to an Illinois-Iowa tour, he remarked, "i am welcomed most kindly by theze warm-hearted people, and my simple 'Milk' iz lapped up az happily az the meat vittles ov the other grate lekturers, who, in common with me, are prowling about this country in sarch ov sassage and reknown" (February 13, 1868, 4).

At Tecumseh, Michigan, he met with such rousing success that he remarked to the *Weekly*, "Never since mi name haz bin Josh Billings, and never since mi "Milk" has flowed, hav i stood up, facing such a torrent ov tumult; sum ov the torrenters aktually laid down on the floor and rolled over; mi heart beat on both sides ov me, and I wouldn't hav stopped till I got through the lektur tu hav took the nominashun for President at the hands of the grate demokratick party ov Amerika" (February 27, 1868, 6). A Pittsburgh, Pennsylvania, audience was so ecstatic over his lecture on "Natral History" that Shaw wondered if he were in a camp meeting and had "struk sum sudden ile." "Sum shouted, and sum cried, and sum seized themselves bi the hair of their heds..." (December 23, 1869, 2), a reception equalled by the rollicking success of a stop in Ohio in 1868 where, according to the *Seneca Advertiser*, his lecture caused so much merriment that "a peck of buttons were gathered up from the floor on cleaning the hall."[41] His western audiences loved him too, Shaw writing the *Weekly* in 1874, "I lektured two nites at Denver, and both nites were a full blown sukcess, and the nuzepapers were so kind, and so profuse in their friendly kriticisms that it fairly started mi floor timbers to read them" (July 13, 7).

Shaw was likewise ebullient over his financial success. Near the conclusion of the 1867-68 season, he wrote the *Weekly* that he would soon have "more money than I ever had at once in my life" (January 30, 1868, 7). The next month he noted, "Lekturing still continners tew pay; I don't know ov ennything that pays better on the investment" (February 6, 1868, 3). Another time he raves, "I am astonished at my success; money cums into me just az tho it waz mine..." (February 13, 1868, 4).

And he wrote his wife, who had complained of being almost out of money, to forget her troubles: "i am positively ritch, and . . . the lektring bizness this winter will make us happy the rest ov our daze."[42] With royalties from the *Allminax* and lucrative returns from these platform appearances, Shaw indeed became very comfortable financially shortly after 1870.

Unlike some of his fellow lecturers, such as Twain and Ward, Shaw genuinely enjoyed traveling the lecture circuit, despite its hardships. He refused to be daunted by the fatigue and inconveniences of travel, the poor beds, the substandard meals, the sometime callousness of lecture-committee representatives. He thrived on the road, for he loved observing the towns, countryside, and people of new locales. After one successful stay, he wrote the *Weekly*: "This iz what i kall glory on the haff shell, this iz oats, this iz like the molassis kandy ov childhood . . ." (February 27, 1868, 6), a statement that summarizes the zest of his dedication to the platform.

CHAPTER 8

A Word of Appraisal

I *Shaw and the Critics: The Nineteenth Century*

NINETEENTH-CENTURY criticism established patterns of thought about Shaw and his fellow literary comedians which have continued to be twentieth-century strongholds, although our own century has also opened up some new approaches. On the unfavorable side, New England *literati* scorned Shaw as being subliterary and feared the harm his "Joshbillingsgate" would inflict on the language.[1] E. C. Stedman accused Shaw and other humorists of causing "the present *horrible* degeneracy of the public taste"; and they decried the fact that American newspapers were "flooded, deluged, swamped, beneath a muddy tide of slang, vulgarity, inartistic bathers, impertinence and buffoonery that is not wit."[2] Others, such as English critic Andrew Lang and Scotsman John Nichol, felt that Shaw simply made little or no contributions to American humor.[3] Mark Twain, Shaw's own friend, in looking back at his fellow platform companions in 1906, lamented their passing but believed they did not last because they were only comedians. Had they "preached," Twain felt, their reputations would have endured,[4] a remark revealing an obvious oversight on Twain's part. No one "preached" more than Shaw.

By far the majority of nineteenth-century popular and literary criticism, however, showed its enjoyment of Shaw and exhibited faith in what he was doing for American humor and morality. As Blair has pointed out, since Shaw's humor was "not so localized or so individualized as a Downing ... or a Major Jones,"[5] his appeal was broad. He communicated with the New England farmer, the middle western city denizen, and the president of

120

the United States. Lincoln, to whom Shaw's brand of humor was appropriately geared, loved his wit and read his aphorisms and the mule essay to his Cabinet.[6] So close were Shaw and Lincoln in comic flair that E. P. Hingston, Ward's lecture manager, once believed Lincoln to be the author of Shaw's works.[7]

Nineteenth-century critics generally lauded Shaw's brand of humor, appreciating its effective drollery, its wit, its pungent insights, its satire, and its sheer funniness.[8] Shaw's contemporary, Gerald Massey, alluded to Shaw's "dry caustic cynicism" and then spoke of his having "a touch of a kind of humor that in itself is inexpressible, in its character indescribable, in its appeal helplessly ludicrous."[9] Shaw's combined wit and humor was the subject of many critical reactions. British critic Robert Ford dubbed him "a Jacques and a Touchstone in one and the same person";[10] a London *Spectator* reviewer gave him the tag "The American Montaigne";[11] while Charles H. Smith called him "Aesop and Ben Franklin, condensed and abridged."[12] His "rare knowledge of human nature," to quote Joel Benton,[13] was considered a major reason for his popularity.

The *Hamilton Literary Monthly* wrote that his popularity on both sides of the Atlantic and with "the peasant and the scholar," as well as with the "kings of thought and the lovers of hearty laughter," was accounted for by the fact that "much valuable wisdom" is couched under his "ingenious cacography" and emphasized that "his rich vein of humor leads always to richer veins of hard, unalloyed common sense."[14] The *Boston Journal* doubted " 'if there can be found in all the realm of eccentricity and individuality more absolute an oddity, more original an author, who has given vent to more common sense, clothed in taking and interesting garb than this same Josh Billings.' "[15] French reviewer Thérèse Bentzon, writing in the *Revue des Deux Mondes* on "Les Humoristes Américains," singled out the moral earnestness and sententiousness at the heart of Shaw's aphorisms and proverbs, couched in humor as these traits are.[16] Finally, George Washington Cable even preferred Shaw's humor to Twain's because he found Shaw more in the tradition of the wise court fool of former days and appreciated the fact that his humor is "fun from first to last" while Twain's must be followed clear through before all the humor is evident. Also

Cable preferred the more dominant moral tone in Shaw's writings.[17]

Although Shaw's wit and humor were obviously the traits most singled out by critics for comment, occasionally other subjects caused reactions. Francis S. Smith was only one of several appraisers who spoke of Shaw's being a widely read and knowledgeable man, despite the impression his seemingly unlettered viewpoint gives.[18] His wisdom, one that obviously reached well beyond the impromptu musings of the cracker-barrel and fireside traditions, was especially appreciated by those who recognized Shaw's intellectual ties with the realm of Western world literature and philosophy. Smith also introduced a view propounded by Max Eastman in the twentieth century that there is something of the poet in Shaw. A minor poet himself, Smith referred to Shaw as a "Natural born poet" and told of turning some of Shaw's prose into verse and being "surprised at the poetical beauty of the picture."[19] As can be seen by Shaw's own venture into poetry (see Chapter 4) as well as his imagistic prose (see Chapters 2 and 3), Smith had isolated a special quality of Shaw's language. It is, in many respects, poetic.

The general esteem in which his own era held Shaw can be seen in numerous regretful remarks concerning his death and disappearance from the literary scene. Perhaps one of the most pointed of these was made by Henry C. Lukens, writing in *Harper's* on American literary comedians that Shaw "is missed all the more because his place yet remains unfilled. Such a heart-searching philosopher, or a speller of like method and graceless aptitude, is rare indeed."[20] This tribute expresses the general sentiment of Shaw's age.

II *Shaw in the Twentieth Century*

Criticism of the first quarter of the twentieth century embarked on the same general trends as that of the preceding century. Critics extolled Shaw's brand of humor and lamented that he was gone, feeling that his place in American humor was still vacant. Joel Benton wrote in 1905: "His career is worthy of more honor than it has thus far received. He was a man of rare good sense, with a decided genius for teaching wholesome truths by epigram."[21] Joseph Lewis French, editor of *Sixty Years of American Humor* and a man who had met Shaw, felt strongly that Shaw "had a great mind, with a well-developed philosophy of life and a genuine gift of turning it all into sheer laughter such as few men of any age or clime have possessed"; and ranked Shaw with James Russell Lowell, saying he shares with Lowell "the laurel of supremacy in the field of American humor."[22] Fred Lewis Pattee praised Shaw for his philosophy and use of aphorisms,[23] while others such as Brander Matthews and William Peterfield Trent singled out his wit and his pungent philosophy, and both men aligned Shaw with La Rochefoucauld.[24]

Among early twentieth-century critical voices that missed Josh Billings after his death were literary historian Carl Holliday, who felt that no nation had "produced during the last half-century a wit surpassing Josh Billings in shrewd sarcasm . . .";[25] Albert Bigelow Paine, who called Shaw "one of the gentlest and loveliest of our pioneers of laughter";[26] and William Dean Howells, who wrote in his "Editor's Easy Chair" column of *Harper's* concerning Shaw and the other platform humorists: "We can only wish that their line may never end. . . . Songs and sermons have been forgotten, but some pleasantry which these kindly fellowmen lodged in our memory keeps their names sweet and dear. We would not undervalue them. . . ."[27]

James Mudge, in his article "A Philosophical Humorist," sums up early twentieth-century critical feeling toward Shaw when he points out that "truth there is here in large abundance, truth expressed with a vigor, a sharpness, and an originality that compel attention." Moreover, Mudge asserts, Shaw "did not write simply to amuse. . . . There was frequently a higher purpose peeping out from among his quaint fancies and odd conceits." In satire, Mudge continues, Shaw "directed his shafts against humbug, pretension, and falsity. He burlesqued the salient weaknesses of the people in a way to set them to thinking, and to doing better. His diagnosis of human nature was an exceedingly shrewd one. He punctured the follies and imbecilities of the multitude with a very keen rapier."[28]

It has been the general trend of later twentieth-century criticism to look with disfavor on or to simply ignore Shaw and his fellow literary comedians. The sophisticated, "enlightened," Realistic age, with its emphasis on belletristic literature has frequently considered the platform comedians as old-fashioned, quaint, and even dull.[29] Shaw's cacography and ungrammatical structures have proved anathema to purists (see below). Shaw and the other comedians have never lost their appeal as literary curiosities, but they have often enjoyed only this dubious place of honor.

Significant exceptions to twentieth-century negativism there have been, however. And considering a number of recent important studies which treat the comedians as writers of merit,[30] a long overdue reevaluation is beginning—an examination that is revealing the multiple talents of these figures and is emphasizing the important contributions these writers made to the rise of Realism in such aspects as subject matter, satire, and diction. Among the critical exceptions, beginning in the 1930's, were favorable reactions by such notables as Will D. Howe, who asserted that Shaw was unsurpassed as lecturer and witty philosopher;[31] George F. Whicher, who praised his "pungent insight";[32] Cyril Clemens, who discussed the universality and pertinence of Shaw's humor;[33] Robert F. Richards, who stated that Shaw had a high degree of wisdom and adeptness at social satire that "raised him above the average word juggler";[34] and Jeannette Tandy, who emphasized what Shaw and Ward did for the common man in America: "The two funny men gave a national presentation and a philosophical interpretation of the common man. They saw the unlettered man of the people on a grander scale than any of his sectional interpreters had ever seen him. And while preserving all his provincial charm and whimsical individuality, they were able to make him, in person and in reputation, a national hero."[35]

Other critics and literary historians have dwelt specifically with Shaw's talents and contributions as a knowledgeable man of letters, a quite valid approach considering the assiduity with which Shaw worked at his writing. Joseph Jones makes the point that Shaw ultimately is far more than a crackerbox philosopher: he is "a rather severely self-disciplined artist."[36] The economy of Shaw's language—the almost poetic concision—has attracted the attentions of several astute observers, such as Walter Blair who lauds him for this "great gift for squeezing much lore into a few words." Instead of concentrating, as did Brown and Locke, on the personalities of their personae, Shaw "gave much time to his [Josh's] way of boiling down thoughts."[37] Blair and Max Eastman both agree that Shaw was an early poetic imagist—Eastman calling him the "father of imagism."[38] It is their belief that this trait signifies the main difference between Shaw and the other humorists in the composition of the aphorism.[39]

On the subject of Shaw as humorist, several twentieth-century critics have been highly incisive. Max Eastman believes that Shaw was effective as a humorist because he, along with Twain, was cognizant of and possessed the two strains that gave American humor its distinct flavor: "the vigor of imagination and the mature enjoyment of nonsense."[40] Jesse Bier, in the most recent exhaustive study of American humor, writes that Shaw and Bret Harte were "our first tentative comic theoreticians," and Bier quotes extensively from Shaw's observations on the craft of humor.[41] Joseph Jones states that Shaw excelled in humor because of his dedication to the art and discipline in the practice of it, "just as every superior humorist is disciplined by the exacting regulations of the craft."[42] Jones then indicates that Shaw's esthetic orientation and approach are emphasized by his avoidance of most of the stock comic devices of his age.[43] Besides the illiterate spelling and occasionally ungrammatical sentences—the former of which Shaw adopted against his will—there are few other poses. Shaw does not caricature politicians—his model is Man; he refrains from insisting on the character of Josh Billings and instead stands "upon the merit of what he says rather than upon any painfully manufactured version of himself." Finally, Jones says, it is the impersonal quality, "sometimes approaching the awful impersonality of Swift," that separates Shaw from his compatriots and aligns him with Mark Twain.[44]

III *The Matter of Spelling*

Shaw originally used the device of cacography to gain popularity. Artemus Ward had found it profitable, and Shaw followed suit with his "Essa on the Muel" and found himself suddenly successful.[45] He never really enjoyed the mode, however; he felt apologetic about it and later regretted that he ever employed it:

I adopted it in a moment ov karlessness, and like a slip in chastity, the world dont let me bak tew grace agin.

Thare iz no moral buty in it, no phisikal force in it, thare iz no humor even in more than one word out ov 16 hundred spelt rong, and iz too small a proporshun tew pay.

All that i kan do in the premises i am willing tew do, and like other sinners who ask for forgiveness and keep rite on sinning, i now ask the world tew forgiv me and i will promis not tew reform.

If others think thare iz enny force or phun in bad spelling i pity them.

Thare iz just az mutch joke in bad spelling az thare iz in looking kross-eyed, and no more.

I hope no one hereafter who takes up literature in enny ov its branches for a living, or for rekreashun, will ever be so lost tew reason or tew phun, az tew spell rong on purpose.[46]

He even spoke facetiously of his reason for beginning to write in this fashion: "The misfortune waz, that the fust piece i wrote for the publik eye, i waz so ashamed ov that i dare not trust it to good spelling, and so did it in bad to hide, and the piece waz lucky, having a run, and i kept on in the way ov wickedness and distorshun."[47]

This technique of misspelling, above all other devices that Shaw used, has been a point of contention with critics from the time of Shaw's own critical reaction against it to the present. Most have deplored it. Among Shaw's contemporaries, Edith Thomson called it a "weak prop,"[48] while Gerald Massey elaborated: "It must be merely from imitation that Josh Billings has adopted his mode of spelling. It does not in the least enrich his humour, has no affinities to it. In the case of Artemus Ward, we may imagine it to be a part of the speaker's character. With him it looks like an element in that species of drollery which is his *forte;* it helps to elongate and *drawl* out the humour. But many of Josh Billings' sayings are keen enough for the short, sharp, direct utterance of Douglas Jerrold, and the spelling is an annoying obstruction. . . ."[49] Even a critic in the literary magazine of Shaw's alma mater asked the pointed question, "Where is the sense of misspelling a fine sentence, whose wit can be appreciated only by those to whom the bad spelling is a cause of disgust?"[50]

In the twentieth century, Fred Lewis Pattee—though blaming the cacography not on Shaw but his times, which "demanded misspelling and clownishness"—still finds the technique damaging. Shaw, he believes, was essentially a philosopher and thus should not have resorted to couching his observations in quaint forms.[51] In an even stronger stand, Albert Bigelow Paine wrote that Shaw was a "genuine smiling philosopher, who might have built up a more permanent and serious reputation had he not been induced to disfigure his maxims with ridiculous spelling. . . ." Paine felt that even Shaw's humorous aphorisms "lose value in that degraded spelling."[52] Finally, and most recently, Jesse Bier objects to the misspelling on grounds of its having no consistency in its forms.[53]

Other reactions have been highly positive to Shaw's chosen mode. Bill Arp believed that the misspelling "spiced his maxims and proverbs, and made them attractive."[54] Joel Benton thought it an "accessory to, or advertisement of" Shaw's wit.[55] To George W. Cable the technique—though not altogether fortunate—was nevertheless "the vehicle of that quality of playfulness so necessary to a humorist."[56] Max Eastman, who offers an understanding view of the technique, implores: "Let us remember that in those days 'correct' spelling was a comparatively recent invention—spelling having been an adventure for everybody in the seventeenth century—and playful bad spelling was a new and natural delight."[57]

It is evident, in reading Shaw, that the cacography serves a definite function, even though it does add a quaintness that has brought disfavor to him from many critics. If it bothers the modern reader, he must remember with Max Eastman that "distorted words can be funny of themselves when presented in the condition called mirth,"[58] and with Jeannette Tandy who points out that, in some of Shaw's more pedestrian utterances, the spelling "is the only novelty."[59] One can hardly deny that the spelling itself is a vital part of the comic effect in such lines as these from "Josh Billings on the Mule": "The mule is haf hoss, and haf Jackass, and then kums tu a full stop, natur diskovering her mistake. . . . The only wa tu keep them [mules] into a paster, is tu turn them into a medder jineing, and let them jump out" (*Sayings,* 13). Along with the occasional distorted syntax and word tricks in Shaw's sentences, the misspellings catch the eye and lend continual surprise with a sustained incongruity that lies at the very basis of comedy itself.

Even if taste dictates more esthetic attractions, however, there is still much left for the modern reader of Shaw. One can follow the line taken by Joseph Jones that the incorrect spelling and occasional distorted grammar "are not essential to the final effect." Jones astutely observes that, while Shaw "is not greatly improved by transliteration, the surprising thing is that he is not destroyed by it."[60] There is no better proof of this point than the correctly penned sayings from the "Uncle Esek's Wisdom" column that Shaw wrote for the *Century*. The droll humor is readily apparent in lines such as the following:

He who has no enemies has no friends—that he can rely upon.

Debt is a good deal like the old-fashioned wire mouse-trap—the hole to get in is four times as big as the one to get out at.

It may be possible for three persons to keep a secret, provided two of them are dead.

Justice is every man's due, but would ruin most people.[61]

There is much in Shaw, thus, for the reader who enjoys the misspellings; and there is much there for the reader who is willing to pass beyond the cacography to the essential material underneath. Either reader, if perceptive, will assuredly discover much by way of wisdom, entertainment, and artistry.

CHAPTER *9*

Conclusion

IT should be obvious at this point that Henry Wheeler Shaw both fulfilled the role of literary comedian and transcended it. Influenced by Artemus Ward with his quaint spelling, stage techniques, and general literary approach, Shaw was at home in the whole tradition of dry wit characterized by Ward, Nasby, Phoenix, and Twain—a tradition that led to twentieth-century counterpart Will Rogers, among others, who carried on Shaw's manner of having a ready, witty comment about almost any subject. In this comic tradition, Shaw appealed to everyone with homespun tastes from Lincoln to New England farmers.

But there is a side of Shaw that is distinctly separate from this tradition of the literary comedians. Unlike Brown and Locke, as observed earlier, he did not project an image of the persona to an extent that Josh Billings became a personality separate from Shaw. And he differed from Twain and others by remaining in the realm of the essay and epigram instead of turning to comic narration or political commentary. Indeed, something of an older, more classical tradition stands behind Shaw's writings. Throughout his essays, he alludes to many of the standard great writers of Western literary tradition, quoting favorite or appropriate passages to corroborate his points, or commenting on some facet of the art or literary success of renowned authors. His favorite writers, judging from the number of times they or their works are mentioned, were Shakespeare, Dickens, Burns, and Bryant. Of Burns, Shaw exclaimed, "I dew consider him the most Poet that ever lived. I had ruther be the author ov one poum i kno ov, that he rit, than tew be king and queen ov England, and keep a hoss and carriage ...(*Sayings*, 121).

129

Other authors frequently mentioned are Goldsmith, Pope, Gray, Byron, Bunyan, Defoe, and Ben Jonson. In world literature he especially revered Boccaccio, Homer, Virgil, and Ovid. Concerning Homer, Shaw wrote, exaggeratively, "I don't read enny boddy else's poetry but Homer's, upon the same principle that i alwus drink, when it is just as handy, out ov a spring, instead ov the outlet" (*Ice*, 104). His references to American writers are scarce, mainly including (besides the aforementioned Bryant) Artemus Ward and Mark Twain. But his paraphrasing of some of Benjamin Franklin's (Poor Richard's) maxims is obvious, especially in his aphorisms.

The strong similarity, minus the dialect, to Franklin has been demonstrated by Blair,[1] Cyril Clemens, S. S. Cox, and others. Cox has written: "There is much of Franklin's shrewd, practical humor under the mask of Josh Billings' sayings."[2] Clemens, besides emphasizing the similarities of Josh's *Farmer's Allminax* to *Poor Richard's*, points out that Franklin and Shaw are "surprisingly alike in their outlook on life: at once shrewd, philosophic, and humorous." And he observes that "many of their sayings were not original with them, but they were always greatly bettered by their rugged wit."[3] If one disregards the misspellings, there is a quality and tone to Shaw's sayings that are far more remindful of Franklin, La Rochefoucauld, Bacon, Dryden, Swift, and Pope than those of his fellow funny men. In the essay and sketch he is more in the tradition of Aesop, Addison, and Montaigne than in that of Ward or Phoenix.

Shaw's conception of humor was broader and more classical than the type of folksy, exaggerated comedy usually associated with the literary comedians. Humor reflected his basic philosophy of life: he saw life as essentially pleasurable, and he wanted everyone to experience the pleasure and satisfaction for himself. As he phrased it, "I pin all my faith, hope, and charity upon this one impulse of my nature, and that is, if I could have my way, there would be a smile continually on the face of every human being on God's footstool, and this smile should ever and anon widen into a broad grin."[4]

Humor should, above all, please; it should never discourage or confound. But it is also functional in correcting and informing mankind, and herein lies Shaw's belief in satire. Temperate

in his attacks, Shaw accepted the Addison-Steele position that
wit aids the presentation of morality: it softens the lesson and
amuses the beholder, while at the same time it couches unavoidable truths that hopefully lead to reform. Shaw's enthusiasm for
life urged him to preach for reform—reform, that is, of an individual variety (he was skeptical of reform movements). He em-
braced all life: the animal and insect kingdoms were as fascinating to him as man. He never tired of dwelling on their species
and characteristics and observing the very nature of human life
reflected there. He was Chaucerian in his love of people, their
habits of mind, their customs; just as he was Chaucerian in his
keen perception of how man often seriously errs and destroys
self and others. He readily excused, even found amusement in,
the foibles of mankind; he was chagrined at major flaws that
harmed humanity, and he spoke out against them.

Shaw had no codified, systematic philosophy of life. He himself
said: "I never was logikal. I never waz a kluss kommunion
thinker. I hav dun all mi thinking on the jump, i alwus shute on
the wing, and hav made menny splendid misses, but once in a
while hav brought down mi animal" (*Friend*, 554). He summed
up a lifetime of reactions to his varied experiences with the
remark: "the susceptibility of my nature looked upon most things
in this life as simply a joke."[5] His views were often as unrelated
to any dominant, pervading philosophy of life as were his
aphorisms foreign to a tightly structured paragraph. But he did,
nevertheless, tend to view life with a basic optimism, a Yankee
faith in the capability and perseverance of man, and a humane
tolerance of man's blunders along the way to improvement. He
approached all of life with eagerness and openness and then reflected on it with honest originality. At times he was skeptical,
even occasionally pessimistic: he thought deeply enough to
realize that Creation is not working as smoothly as it should.
But he normally managed to eclipse gloom with an infectious
lightness of heart and a witty remark that convinced his audience
or reader that life was worth it after all. His New England heritage reminded him that the main function of man on earth is to
see to the business of life; Shaw felt it his duty to show man the
more propitious aspects of that function.

It is often difficult to tell the exact extent to which an author,

particularly a minor one, is influential on literary posterity;
but it is obvious that Shaw made his mark. He almost assuredly
asserted a direct influence on twentieth-century humorists Will
Rogers and Kin Hubbard. Hubbard's *Abe Martin's Almanack*
of the 1930's was a throwback to Shaw's in aphorisms, humor,
and dialect.[6] Max Eastman sees in Shaw's picturesque lines the
beginning of Imagism in letters. Jeannette Tandy has stated that
Shaw's prose style may have suggested techniques to "that school
of modern prose whose exponent is Gertrude Stein."[7] Despite
Bernard De Voto's denial of a Shaw influence on Twain,[8] Cyril
Clemens points to the epigrams as chapter headings in *Pudd'n-
head Wilson* and *Following the Equator* as being done "in the
true Billings manner."[9] An anonymous writer in the *Hamilton
Literary Monthly* even introduces Shaw as an influence on the
spelling reform movement of the first decade of the twentieth
century that urged a more phonetic approach: "Poor old 'Josh,'
who has been so long unappreciated and positively ignored, is
bound at last to be canonized in the precious calendar of the
orthographical saints and to become at last a veritable hero. 'Back
to Josh' is the watchword of the present-day spelling-reformers."[10]

Aside from these specific influences, Shaw, along with the
other literary comedians, must be remembered as contributing
to the rise of Realism in the last four decades of the nineteenth
century—a role too often overlooked. Though Shaw's approach is
essentially comic, underneath the comedy are critical barbs as
poignant as those of Twain and as indicting as the attacks of H. L.
Mencken and Sinclair Lewis. V. F. Calverton corroborates this
view when he says that the literary comedians—despite all their
comic devices—"did more to destroy the romantic tradition than
did any of their more dignified literary contemporaries"; and he
stresses that "there was a realistic twist about many of them
which made the people think as well as laugh.[11] Shaw certainly
wanted his readers and hearers to be amused, but he did insist
that they also think. Addison's announced purpose of *The Spectator*—"to enliven morality with wit, and to temper wit with
morality"—speaks for Shaw's aims in humor. He insisted that
man examine his flaws and the general shams and hypocrisies
of life, but he couched his admonitions in wit.

Unfortunately, considering Shaw's qualities, contributions, and

Realistic tendencies, he is currently too much ignored and is considered a literary curiosity. His spelling *is* a curiosity today, of course, and certainly it is a major drawback to his winning wide appeal. But his accomplishments as humorist, satirist, and knowledgeable stylist are significant and should receive more attention than they have. Jesse Bier, in a new, fresh discussion of Shaw and the literary comedians, appraises their achievement as being "a rapid maturity of gift on every side"; and he characterizes their work as being "national in scope" and as astonishing to the modern reader "in its comic energies." Bier's final assessment is that "in the bulk of its work it remains significantly and durably modern."[12] Shaw, in his total contribution, lives up to Bier's appraisal.

Though Shaw dedicated himself as a man of letters to an upstart tradition that inevitably could not continue to arrest the attentions of the majority of readers in a rapidly growing, dynamic country, he was an artist who succeeded to a degree generally unrealized by literary posterity. The achievement of his humor alone is remarkable. Charles Dawson Shanly, a contemporary of Shaw's, points out the discipline and genius necessary to produce successful humor: "Great assiduity is a thing almost incompatible with humorous writing. The strain of always trying to be witty and epigrammatic on the surface, without losing grasp for a moment of the weightier considerations involved, is one against which few minds could contend successfully for long, continuous periods. . . ."[13] Henry Wheeler Shaw's was one of those few minds.

Notes and References

Chapter One

1. Edith Parker Thomson, "The Home of Josh Billings," *New England Magazine*, XIX (February, 1899), 699-701.

2. Cyril Clemens, *Josh Billings: Yankee Humorist* (Webster Groves, Missouri, 1932), p. 2. Hereafter cited in notes as *Josh Billings* to distinguish it from other titles by Clemens.

3. *Ibid.*, p. 9.

4. *Hamilton Literary Monthly*, XVI (September, 1881), 65.

5. Cyril Clemens, *Josh Billings*, p. 13.

6. *Ibid.*, p. 28.

7. See Cyril Clemens, *Josh Billings*, pp. 36-40, for Shaw's diary extracts concerning the trials of the river-boat experience.

8. Edmund Platt, *The Eagle's History of Poughkeepsie* (Poughkeepsie, 1905), p. 204, mentions that Shaw was the auctioneer selected to auction off some valuable school property in Poughkeepsie on November 24, 1865.

9. *Ibid.*, pp. 170-71.

10. *Ibid.*, p. 171.

11. Cyril Clemens, *Josh Billings*, p. 41.

12. *Ibid.*, p. 46.

13. Jennette Tandy, *Crackerbox Philosophers in American Humor and Satire* (New York, 1925), p. 148.

14. Frank Luther Mott, *A History of American Magazines* (Cambridge, Massachusetts, 1938), II, 37.

15. Cyril Clemens, *Josh Billings*, p. 139.

16. Will M. Clemens, *Famous Funny Fellows: Brief Biographical Sketches of American Humorists* (Cleveland, 1882), p. 55.

17. The *Weekly* for November 5, 1868 (p. 4), announced the marriage of Grace Shaw to William Duff.

18. Francis S. Smith, *Life and Adventures of Josh Billings* (New York, 1883), p. 44.

19. William W. Ellsworth, *A Golden Age of Authors* (Boston and New York, [1919]), p. 214.

20. J. B. Pond, *Eccentricities of Genius* (New York, [1900]), p. 187.

21. Charles H. Smith, "Bill Arp on Josh Billings," *The Farm and the Fireside* (Atlanta, 1891), p. 254.

22. Francis S. Smith, pp. 63-64.

23. *Ibid.*, p. 64.

24. Charles H. Smith, pp. 252-53. Carleton arranged a secret meeting, not informing Arp that Shaw would be there. At first Arp mistook Shaw for a Methodist preacher: "He looked like one, a very solemn one. His long hair was parted in the middle and silvered with gray. His face was heavily bearded, his eyes well set and his mouth drooped at the corners" (p. 253).

25. Melville Landon, *Eli Perkins: Thirty Years of Wit* (New York, [1891]), p. 4.

26. Melville Landon, *Kings of the Platform and Pulpit* (New York, 1895), pp. 78-79.

27. *Ibid.*, p. 76.

28. In Philadelphia, February, 1882 (Cyril Clemens, *Josh Billings*, p. 108).

29. *Mark Twain's Autobiography*, ed. Charles Neider (New York, [1959]), p. 182.

30. See Joseph Jones, "Josh Billings Visits a Mark Twain Shrine," *American Notes and Queries*, IV (September, 1944), 83.

31. *Everybody's Friend, or Josh Billings' Encyclopoedia and Proverbial Philosophy of Wit and Humor* (Hartford, 1874), p. 574. Hereafter cited in text as *Friend*.

32. Paul Fatout, *Mark Twain on the Lecture Circuit* (Bloomington, 1960), p. 141.

33. "Sum Biogriphal—Mark Twain," *New York Weekly* (October 6, 1870), p. 7.

34. Cyril Clemens, *Shillaber* (Webster Groves, Missouri, 1946), p. 119.

35. Albert Bigelow Paine, *Th. Nast: His Period and His Pictures* (New York, 1904), p. 277.

36. *Josh Billings' Trump Kards: Blue Grass Philosophy* (New York, 1877), p. 9. An earlier and somewhat different version appeared in the *New York Weekly* (June 23, 1873), p. 4.

37. Will M. Clemens, p. 55.

38. Pond, p. 187.

Chapter Two

1. Hereafter cited in text as *Century* and *Weekly*, respectively.

2. Hereafter cited in text as *Sayings*.

3. Hereafter cited in text as *Ice*.

4. *Josh Billings' Wit and Humor* (London, 1874), an English publication, is identical in contents to *Friend*. Only the pagination is different, the former running to 448 pages as opposed to 617 in *Friend*.

5. Hereafter cited in text as *Works*. The contents and pagination of *Friend* and *Works* are identical through item 256, "Dog Talk." Thereafter, with the exception of nine pieces that appear in both volumes, *Friend* contains some thirty-nine pieces that do not appear in *Works*. Whenever possible I have cited *Works* rather than *Friend* in documenting quotations of aphorisms since it is the volume more available to readers.

6. Landon, *Kings of the Platform and Pulpit*, pp. 76-77.

7. Walter Blair, *Horse Sense in American Humor* (Chicago, [1942]), pp. 226-27.

8. Shaw modified his spelling and grammar in order to satisfy the wishes of Josiah G. Holland, editor, the *Century Magazine* (Ellsworth, p. 213).

9. Frederic Hudson, *Journalism in the United States from 1690 to 1872* (New York, 1873), p. 692.

10. Tandy, p. 94.

11. Jesse Bier, *The Rise and Fall of American Humor* (New York, [1968]), p. 100.

12. As James Mudge points out in "A Philosophical Humorist," *Methodist Review*, CI (March, 1918), 207.

13. Charles H. Smith, p. 252.

14. H. L. Mencken, *The American Language* (New York, 1936), p. 442.

15. Walter Blair, *Native American Humor (1800-1900)* (New York, 1937), p. 121.

16. When not his own, Shaw's sayings are frequently rephrasings of those by Franklin, La Rochefoucauld, Bacon, Dryden, Swift, Pope, Chesterfield, and other notable users of the epigram.

17. Blair, *Native American Humor*, p. 121.

18. Max Eastman, *Enjoyment of Laughter* (New York, 1936), p. 85.

19. *Ibid.*

20. *Ibid.*

21. *Ibid.*, p. 175.

22. *Ibid.*

23. Bier, p. 78.

24. Charles H. Smith, p. 252.

Chapter Three

1. Blair, *Horse Sense in American Humor*, p. 222.
2. "Josh Billings: Some Yankee Notions on Humor," *Studies in English* (Austin, Texas, 1943), p. 149.
3. *Sayings*, pp. 15-16. Shaw's parody includes such questions as "Are yu mail or femail? If so, Pleze state how long you have been so" and "Hav yu ever committed suiside, and if so, how did it seem to affect yu?"
4. G. H. Derby, *Phoenixiana; or, Sketches and Burlesques* (New York, 1856).
5. Bier, p. 115.
6. This observation has been made also by Joseph Jones ("Josh Billings: Some Yankee Notions of Humor," p. 160).
7. Blair, *Horse Sense in American Humor*, p. 226.
8. Charles H. Smith, p. 252.
9. See *Sayings*, pp. 133-36; *Ice*, pp. 205-9 (and *Weekly*, October 17, 1867, p. 7); *Works* (and *Friend*), pp. 396-400, 424-27; *Trump Kards*, p. 29 (and for an extended version of the same, *Weekly*, September 24, 1868, p. 8).
10. *Sayings*, pp. 186-88, 205-7; *Ice*, pp. 66-71; *Friend*, pp. 526-28; *Works* (and *Friend*), pp. 424-27.
11. See *Works* (and *Friend*), pp. 386-89, 428-29.

Chapter Four

1. *Weekly* (June 16, 1873), p. 8. A shorter, later version of the same appears in *Trump Kards*, p. 45.
2. The poem first appeared in the *Weekly* on October 12, 1871, p. 4. It was reprinted in *Friend* (and *Works*), pp. 390-93.

Chapter Five

1. These volumes sold for ten cents with the exception of *Josh Billings' Spice Box*, some issues of which brought twenty-five cents a copy.
2. "A Brief History of American Jest Books," *Bulletin of the New York Public Library*, XLVII (April, 1943), 273.
3. *Ibid.*
4. For details see Walter Blair, "The Popularity of Nineteenth-Century American Humorists," *American Literature*, III (May, 1931), 178-85; Ernest L. Hancock, "The Passing of the American Comic," *The Bookman*, XXII (September, 1905), 78-84; Brander Matthews, "The Comic Periodical Literature of the United States," *American*

Bibliopolist, VII (August, 1875), 199-201; and Frank Luther Mott, *A History of American Magazines* (Cambridge, 1938), III, 263-74.

5. The exact number of *Spice Box* issues is undetermined. The first seems to have appeared in 1874 and is advertised in the *New York Weekly* as "THIRTY-SIX PAGES of genuine Fun . . . , especially adapted for RAILROAD READING," published at twenty-five cents a copy by Street & Smith Publishers (June 29, 1874, p. 7). Cyril Clemens lists another issue under the date 1882, the publisher being G. W. Carleton. Another number is a fifty-page volume published by J. S. Ogilvie & Co., New York (date unknown), a producer of "railroad literature," cheap humor, and sensational fiction from 1843 to 1910. It is this issue I have in my collection and refer to in my discussion.

6. The pages measure 26½ x 18 cm, whereas Shaw's other jest books are small with pages of 18 x 12 cm. Undoubtedly the larger size as well as the increased length of *Spice Box* is due to its being intended for reading while in transit on railways.

7. Only two bear signatures: one is signed "T. Worth," identifiable as Thomas Worth, noted graphic humorist of the day, and undoubtedly others are by him also. The initials "SMS" appear on one other, but whom they represent is unknown.

8. Frederick Stuart Church was a popular illustrator who, among other contributions, co-illustrated the first edition of Joel Chandler Harris' *Uncle Remus* (1880).

9. Weiss, p. 286.

10. The only copy known extant is in the Harvard College Library.

11. The illustrations in *Cook Book* are by Livingston Hopkins, New York free-lance artist who also illustrated *Josh Billings' Farmer's Allminax, Old Probability,* and *Josh Billings Struggling With Things.*

12. This piece is a different "Hash" from that in *Trump Kards.*

13. See note 11 above.

Chapter Six

1. For the somewhat inconsistent publication facts see Blair, "The Popularity of Nineteenth-Century American Humorists," p. 187; Cyril Clemens, *Josh Billings,* p. 115; Mott, III, 248; F. S. Smith, p. 43; and Tandy, p. 149. Mott lists the *Allminax* among the best sellers of the day, ranking it in range of circulation with some of the outstanding novels (III, 247).

2. For the best historical accounts of the almanac in America see Clarence S. Brigham, ["An Account of American Almanacs and Their Value for Historical Study"], *Proceedings of the American Anti-*

quarian Society, XXXV (1925), 194-209; N. W. Lovely, "Notes
on New England Almanacs," *New England Quarterly,* VIII (June,
1935), 264-77; Charles L. Nichols, "Notes on the Almanacs of
Massachusetts," *Proceedings of the American Antiquarian Society,*
XXII (April, 1912), 15-134; and Henry M. Robinson, "The Almanac,"
The Bookman, LXXV (June-July, 1932), 218-24.

3. As Clarence S. Brigham has pointed out, the early almanac
was instrumental in shaping the morals of the people. "The exhorta-
tions to frugality, temperance, industry, and piety and upright
living must have had a permanent influence. . . ." The use of proverbs
interspersed with weather predictions for the individual months
got its start in the late seventeenth century, and people found these
sayings particularly meaningful and memorable because they were
phrased in a pleasing and catching way (["An Account of American
Almanacs . . ."], p. 197).

4. The Man of the Signs (*Homo Signorum*) was frequently displayed on almanac pages to please readers interested in the influence
of the stars on the body. Even though many of the almanac makers
themselves did not believe in what the emblem represents, their
audience largely did, and these men were business-minded enough
to give their readers what they wanted. For a thorough discussion
of the Man of the Signs see George Lyman Kittredge, *The Old
Farmer and His Almanack* (Cambridge, 1920), [New York, 1967],
pp. 53-61.

5. For an excellent, detailed discussion of this specialization see
Brigham, ["An Account of American Almanacs . . ."], pp. 198-205.

6. Constance Rourke, *American Humor: A Study of the National
Character* (New York, 1931), p. 237.

7. This practice was a feature, for example, of the quite early
John Tulley's Almanack for 1768 and *Roger Sherman's Almanack
for 1750* (see Lovely, "Notes on New England Almanacs," pp.
267-68).

8. See Rourke, p. 237.

9. "Notes on the Almanacs of Massachusetts," p. 38.

10. See William Murrell, *A History of American Graphic Humor*
(New York, 1938), I, 154, and Weiss, "A Brief History of American
Jest Books," pp. 280-81, for listings.

11. Weiss, p. 281.

12. For examples of the jokes see Weiss, pp. 281-82.

13. Murrell, I, 154.

14. See James H. Fitts, "The Thomas Almanacs," *Essex Institute
Historical Collections,* XII (October, 1874), 263, and Nichols, "Notes
on the Almanacs of Massachusetts," pp. 44-134.

15. The best discussions of Thomas' life, career, and death are found in Fitts, "The Thomas Almanacs"; Kittredge, *The Old Farmer and His Almanac*; and Robinson, "The Almanac."

16. For discussions of the character sketches see Kittredge, pp. 86-97, and Tandy, pp. 13-14.

17. According to Francis S. Smith, Shaw's illness caused him to return to New York where he wrote the rough draft (pp. 41-42); Cyril Clemens says he stayed in Maine as a patient in a farmhouse and there wrote the work (*Josh Billings,* pp. 114-15). On other details of its composition, however, Smith and Clemens are in agreement. It is to these two sources I am indebted for my discussion of the launching of Shaw's almanac.

18. Cyril Clemens, *Josh Billings,* p. 115.

19. Landon, *Kings of the Platform and Pulpit,* p. 95, and F. S. Smith, p. 44.

20. See Kittredge, pp. 56, 40, respectively.

21. From December, 1873.

22. Tandy, p. 149.

23. Cyril Clemens, *Josh Billings,* p. 128.

24. VIII (September, 1873), 57.

25. (November 24, 1873), p. 7.

26. (October 12, 1874), p. 7.

27. A remark made by Twain in the Buffalo *Express.* Quoted by Milton Meltzer, *Mark Twain Himself* (New York, [1960]), pp. 116-17.

Chapter Seven

1. In Millbury, Massachusetts. See Cecil B. Hayes, *The American Lyceum: Its History and Contribution to Education* (Washington, 1932), pp. xi, 2. In my discussion of the lecture system in America I am mainly indebted to this earliest account of the lyceum. Also important is the later, more detailed discussion by Carl Bode, *The American Lyceum* (New York, 1956).

2. Cyril Clemens, *Josh Billings,* p. 65. I am indebted to both Clemens' biography (pp. 65-86) and F. S. Smith's (pp. 45-55) for my discussion of Shaw's rise as a lecturer.

3. Clemens, *ibid.,* pp. 68-69.

4. F. S. Smith, p. 54, and Clemens, *ibid.,* p. 72.

5. Pond, p. 536.

6. *Mark Twain's Autobiography,* ed. Charles Neider, p. 176.

7. Fatout, p. 103.

8. E. P. Hingston, *The Genial Showman* (London, 1871), pp. 120-21.

9. See Chapter 1 for details.

10. A. B. Paine, *Mark Twain: A Biography* (New York, 1912), II, 444-45.

11. F. S. Smith, p. 55.

12. Cyril Clemens, *Josh Billings*, p. 73.

13. According to the *Hamilton Literary Monthly*, XIV (January, 1880), 216.

14. Mentioned in a letter by Shaw quoted in Will M. Clemens, p. 52.

15. "Milk," *Weekly* (October 13, 1873), p. 4.

16. See the *Weekly* (September 1, 1873), p. 8.

17. According to Shaw's account of it in the *Weekly* (August 4, 1873), p. 4—reprinted in *Friend*, pp. 584-89.

18. *Weekly* (October 13, 1873), p. 4.

19. Reprinted in Landon, *Kings of the Platform and Pulpit*, pp. 80-94.

20. *Ibid.*, p. 81.

21. *Weekly* (August 4, 1873), p. 4, and *Friend*, p. 585.

22. ["Milk"], Landon, *Kings of the Platform and Pulpit*, p. 82.

23. Will M. Clemens, p. 55.

24. Shaw wrote to a lecture committee representative: "I don't have enny thing tew aktually say about *milk* in this lektur, it was thought best tew call it sumthing after it was huddled together, and i picked out the stillist name i could find" (*Friend*, p. 502). Occasionally when before an audience he did refer to the milk present on the table. Once holding up the glass, he quipped, "The best thing I know on milk is . . . . . . cream!" (Cyril Clemens, *Josh Billings*, p. 107). Jesse Bier sees the milk hoax as part of the general tendency of the platform humorists toward parody, a reflection of their critical, skeptical reactions to life (pp. 111-12).

25. Landon, *Kings of the Platform and Pulpit*, p. 80.

26. *Ibid.*

27. *Ibid.*

28. Will M. Clemens, p. 54.

29. Stephen Leacock, *The Greatest Pages of American Humor* (Garden City, [1936]), p. 84.

30. Eastman, p. 55.

31. Paine, II, 444-45.

32. Also see *Friend*, p. 507.

33. *Weekly* (June 22, 1874), p. 4.

34. "What I Kno About Hotels," *Weekly* (September 1, 1873), p. 8; *Friend*, p. 603.

35. "Advice Tew Lectur Kommittys," *Weekly* (July 8, 1872),

p. 4; *Friend* and *Works*, pp. 373-76. Cf. "About Lekturing," *Weekly* (April 9, 1877), p. 3.

36. "Hints to Comik Lekturers," *Weekly* (March 30, 1871), p. 8; *Friend* and *Works*, pp. 89-92.

37. *Weekly* (February 10, 1870), p. 3; *Friend*, p. 494.

38. *Ibid.*

39. Shaw would have had to leave his family behind, reportedly because his two daughters wished to remain in school (Cyril Clemens, *Josh Billings*, p. 73).

40. "Josh on a Lekturing Raid," *Weekly* (January 30, 1868), p. 7.

41. David Mead, *Yankee Eloquence in the Middle West: The Ohio Lyceum 1850-1870* (East Lansing, 1951), p. 233.

42. The letter is summarized in *Weekly* (February 27, 1868), p. 6.

Chapter Eight

1. James R. Aswell, ed., *Native American Humor* (New York, [1947]), p. 394. Frank Luther Mott also points out that whereas English critics found the new American humorists funny, American critics were generally supercilious toward them (III, 264).

2. Laura Stedman and George M. Gould, ed., *Life and Letters of Edmund Clarence Stedman* (New York, 1910), I, 477.

3. Lang ranks him with Kerr rather than with Ward or Twain, saying that most of his humor is in his misspelling (*Lost Leaders*, London, 1892, p. 181). Nichol thought very little of American humor in general and felt Shaw's satire is generally "of a minor description" (*American Literature, An Historical Sketch*, Edinburgh, 1885, pp. 424-26).

4. *The Autobiography of Mark Twain*, ed. Charles Neider, pp. 297-98.

5. Blair, *Horse Sense in American Humor*, pp. 221-22.

6. Joel Benton, *Persons and Places* (New York, 1905), p. 110, and Cyril Clemens, *Josh Billings*, pp. 129-30, 132.

7. Nichol, p. 423.

8. Edith Parker Thomson, for example, discusses the pure humor in Shaw ("The Home of Josh Billings," p. 698), and S. S. Cox speaks of Shaw's "species of drollery which even our English reviewers have begun to appreciate . . ." ("American Humor," *Harper's Magazine*, LXXX [April, May, 1875], 698).

9. "Yankee Humor," *Quarterly*, CXXII (January, 1867), 224.

10. *American Humorists* (London, 1897), p. 61.

11. See *Hamilton Literary Monthly*, IX (October, 1874), 120.

12. Charles H. Smith, p. 252.

13. "Reminiscences of Eminent Lecturers," *Harper's Magazine,* XCVI (March, 1898), 610.

14. XIII (February, 1879), 268.

15. Quoted in *Hamilton Literary Monthly,* XIX (February, 1885), 234.

16. CCIV (August 15, 1872), 853-55. An English translation of the article appears in the *New York Weekly* for June 2, 1873, p. 4.

17. See Joseph Jones, "Josh Billings: Some Yankee Notions on Humor," pp. 156-57; and Arlin Turner, *George W. Cable: A Biography* (Durham, 1956), p. 44.

18. F. S. Smith, p. 65.

19. *Ibid.*

20. LXXX (April, 1890), 796.

21. Benton, p. 111.

22. Joseph L. French, *Sixty Years of American Humor* (Boston, 1924), p. 15.

23. F. L. Pattee, *A History of American Literature Since 1870* (New York, 1915), p. 41.

24. Matthews, *The American of the Future and Other Essays* (New York, 1909), p. 170; Trent, "A Retrospect of American Humor," *Century,* LXIII (November, 1901), 50.

25. Carl Holiday, *Wit and Humor of Colonial Days* (Philadelphia and London, 1912), p. 5.

26. Paine, II, 445.

27. CXXXIV (February, 1917), 442.

28. P. 208.

29. Walter Blair, though recognizing certain contributions, views Shaw as an old-fashioned humorist even in his own day (*Horse Sense in American Humor,* pp. 219, 228). Kenneth S. Lynn omits both Nasby and Billings from *The Comic Tradition in America* (London, 1958), because he finds them "dull" (p. xi).

30. For example, James C. Austin, *Artemus Ward* (New York, [1964]), and *Petroleum V. Nasby* (New York, [1965]); Jesse Bier, "Literary Comedians," in *The Rise and Fall of American Humor* (1968); and John M. Harrison, *The Man Who Made Nasby, David Ross Locke* (Chapel Hill, [1969]).

31. "Early Humorists," *Cambridge History of American Literature* (New York, 1931), II, 157.

32. "Minor Humorists," *ibid.,* III, 30.

33. Cyril Clemens, *Josh Billings,* p. 171.

34. Robert F. Richards, *Concise Dictionary of American Literature* (New York, [1955]), p. 16.

35. Tandy, p. 157.

36. "Josh Billings: Some Yankee Notions on Humor," p. 156.

37. Blair, *Horse Sense in American Humor,* p. 227.

38. Eastman, p. 175. See my Chapter 2 for a discussion of Eastman on Shaw's Imagism.

39. As Blair emphasizes, "It may be true that, more than other creators of proverbs—the literary ones, at any rate—Josh had a habit of getting his ideas into picture form . . ." (*Horse Sense in American Humor,* p. 228).

40. Eastman, p. 174.

41. Bier, p. 115.

42. "Josh Billings: Some Yankee Notions on Humor," p. 156.

43. *Ibid.,* p. 158.

44. *Ibid.*

45. See Chapter 1 for details.

46. "Answers to Personal Letters," *Weekly* (June 23, 1873), p. 4.

47. *Ibid.*

48. "The Home of Josh Billings," p. 699.

49. "Yankee Humor," p. 224.

50. *Hamilton Literary Monthly,* IX (October, 1874), p. 120.

51. Pattee, p. 42.

52. Paine, II, 445.

53. Bier, p. 98.

54. C. H. Smith, p. 252.

55. "Reminiscences of Eminent Lecturers," p. 110.

56. "Drop Shot," *New Orleans Daily Picayune* (July 17, 1870). Quoted by Joseph Jones, "Josh Billings: Some Yankee Notions on Humor," p. 157.

57. Eastman, p. 135.

58. *Ibid.*

59. Tandy, p. 152.

60. "Josh Billings: Some Yankee Notions on Humor," p. 159.

61. The first two sayings are from XXXVI (June, 1888), 2; quote three from XXXVI (July, 1888), 478; and four from XXXVI (August, 1888), 799.

Chapter Nine

1. Blair, *Horse Sense in American Humor,* pp. 14-16.

2. "American Humor," p. 698.

3. Cyril Clemens, *Josh Billings,* p. 168.

4. Will M. Clemens, p. 51.

5. *Ibid.,* p. 50.

6. As Blair has pointed out (*Horse Sense in American Humor,* p. 258).

7. Tandy, p. 151.

8. Bernard De Voto, *Mark Twain's America* (Boston, 1932), p. 219.

9. Cyril Clemens, *Josh Billings*, p. 169.

10. XL (March, 1906), 283.

11. V. F. Calverton, *The Liberation of American Literature* (New York, 1932), pp. 318-19.

12. Bier, p. 116.

13. "Comic Journalism," *Atlantic Monthly*, XIX (February, 1867), 167.

Selected Bibliography

PRIMARY SOURCES

Aside from the entries below, two important repositories of Shaw's published writings are the *New York Weekly*, May 30, 1867–October 27, 1888 (exact terminal date uncertain), Shaw's columns bearing the titles "The Josh Billings' Papers," "Josh Billings' Spice Box," and "Josh Billings' Philosophy"; and the *Century Magazine*, XXVII (March, 1884)–XXXVI (August, 1888), Shaw's aphorisms of "Uncle Esek" appearing in the "Bric-a-brac" section.

Josh Billings, Hiz Sayings. New York: G. W. Carleton & Co., 1865.
Josh Billings on Ice and Other Things. New York: G. W. Carleton & Co., 1868.
Twelve Ansestrals Sighns in the Billings' Zodiac Gallery. New York: G. W. Carleton & Co. (?), 1873.
Everybody's Friend, or Josh Billings' Encyclopoedia and Proverbial Philosophy of Wit and Humor. Hartford: American Publishing Co., 1874.
Josh Billings' Spice Box. New York: G. W. Carleton & Co., Street & Smith Publishers, J. S. Ogilvie & Co., 1874 and following [an undetermined number of issues published by these companies].
Josh Billings' Wit and Humor. London: George Routledge and Sons, 1874.
Complete Comical Writings of Josh Billings. New York: G. W. Carleton & Co., 1876.
Josh Billings' Trump Kards: Blue Grass Philosophy. New York: G. W. Carleton & Co., 1877.
Old Probability: Perhaps Rain—Perhaps Not. New York: G. W. Carleton & Co., 1879.
Josh Billings' Cook Book and Picktorial Proverbs. New York: G. W. Carleton & Co., 1880.
Josh Billings Struggling with Things. New York: G. W. Carleton & Co., 1881.
The Complete Works of Josh Billings. New York: G. W. Dillingham Co., 1888.
Josh Billings' Old Farmer's Allminax, 1870-1879. New York: G. W. Dillingham Co., 1902.

Selections from the Writings of Josh Billings, or: Proverbial Philosophy of Wit and Humor. Introduction by Carl Purlington Rollins. Athens, Georgia: K. De Renne, 1940.

SECONDARY SOURCES

Only a few articles and books of biographical-critical nature are exclusively devoted to Henry Wheeler Shaw. I have included in the following list, therefore, numerous works which discuss Shaw among other subjects; but I have limited my selection to those studies that contain important and incisive remarks.

ASWELL, JAMES R., ed. *Native American Humor.* New York: Harper & Brothers, [1947]. Anthology of American humor with selections from Shaw's writings and a brief biographical-critical sketch.

BENTON, JOEL. *Persons and Places.* New York: Broadway Publishing Co., 1905. Includes a few biographical facts and a brief but appreciative view of Shaw's humor and wit.

————. "Reminiscences of Eminent Lecturers," *Harper's,* XCVI (March, 1898), 603-14. Brief mention of Shaw's lecture success and his rare knowledge of human nature.

BENTZON, THÉRÈSE. "Les Humoristes Américains, II, Artemus Ward, —Josh Billings,—Hans Breitman," *Revue des Deux Mondes,* CCIV (August 15, 1872), 837-62. Appreciative view of Shaw; considers him unequalled in native humor and comic zeal. Discusses his philosophical bent.

BIER, JESSE. *The Rise and Fall of American Humor.* New York: Holt, Rinehart and Winston, 1968. Important reevaluation of Shaw and the literary comedians; emphasizes their contributions to the rise of Realism; points out Shaw's pioneering efforts in the realm of comic theory.

BLAIR, WALTER. *Horse Sense in American Humor.* Chicago: The University of Chicago Press, [1942]. Somewhat shortsightedly fits Shaw into an "old-fashioned" tradition of American humor, but shows insight into the special traits of his essays and aphorisms.

————. *Native American Humor (1800-1900).* New York: American Book Co., 1937. Only sporadic references to Shaw; contains helpful bibliography and two selections from Shaw's writings.

BLANKENSHIP, RUSSELL. *American Literature as an Expression of the National Mind.* New York: Henry Holt and Company, [1949]. Shaw's achievement in the aphorisms discussed and praised.

BROOKS, VAN WYCK. *The Times of Melville and Whitman.* [New

York]: E. P. Dutton & Co., Inc., 1947. Few interesting, if occasionally inaccurate, facts about Shaw's life and an appreciative view of his originality.

CALVERTON, V. F. *The Liberation of American Literature.* New York: Charles Scribner's Sons, 1932. Links Shaw with other nineteenth-century humorists who contributed heavily to the demise of Romanticism and ushered in the "realistic challenge."

CLEMENS, CYRIL. "Josh Billings: A Neglected Humorist," *Overland Monthly,* XIIC (January, 1934), 12. Statement of the unfortunate critical neglect of Shaw and a brief sampling of his works.

————. *Josh Billings, Yankee Humorist.* Webster Groves, Missouri: International Mark Twain Society, 1932. Standard biography with valuable bibliography of primary and secondary works.

————. *Shillaber.* Webster Groves, Missouri: International Mark Twain Society, 1946. Contains a reference to the Shaw-Shillaber friendship.

CLEMENS, SAMUEL L. *Mark Twain's Library of Humor.* Ed. William D. Howells and Charles H. Clark. New York: Charles L. Webster & Co., 1888. Anthology containing six of Shaw's essays and numerous aphorisms.

————. *The Autobiography of Mark Twain.* Ed. Charles Neider. New York: Harper & Row Publishers, Inc., 1959. Offers a glimpse of the Shaw-Twain-Nasby friendship while the three were fellow lecturers with Redpath's Bureau. Has a few other comments on Shaw.

CLEMENS, WILL M. *Famous Funny Fellows, Brief Biographical Sketches of American Humorists.* Cleveland: William W. Williams, 1882. Helpful biographical sketch of Shaw containing obscure facts and a general view of his accomplishments.

COX, S. S. "American Humor," *Harper's Magazine,* LXXX (April-May, 1875), 690-702; 847-59. Brief description of Shaw's comic technique and an appreciation of his brand of drollery, though his accomplishments are deemed subliterary.

DAY, DONALD. *Uncle Sam's Uncle Josh.* Boston: Little, Brown and Company, [1953]. Anthology of representative selections from Shaw's writings.

EASTMAN, MAX. "Humor and America." *The Enjoyment of Laughter.* New York: Simon & Schuster, 1936. Important for pointing out the poetic characteristics of Shaw's writing—especially the imagery—and discussing Shaw's ideas on humor.

ELLSWORTH, WILLIAM W. *A Golden Age of Authors: A Publisher's Recollections.* Boston and New York: Houghton Mifflin Co.,

1919. Insight into Shaw's contribution to the *Century Magazine* as "Uncle Esek."

FATOUT, PAUL. *Mark Twain on the Lecture Circuit.* Bloomington: Indiana University Press, 1960. References to Shaw as a member of Redpath's Bureau and his connections with Twain.

FORD, ROBERT. *American Humorists.* London: A. Gardner, 1897. Contains a sketch of Shaw as humorist-satirist; numerous excerpts from his writings.

FRENCH, JOSEPH L. *Sixty Years of American Humor.* Boston: Little, Brown and Co., 1924. Anthology of American humor containing four selections from Shaw; introductory appraisal of his contributions; compares his excellence in humor with James Russell Lowell's.

GRIMES, GEOFFREY ALLAN. " 'Muels,' 'Owls,' and Other Things: Folk Material in the Tobacco Philosophy of Josh Billings," *New York Folklore Quarterly,* XXVI (December, 1970), 283-96. Relates Shaw's use of exaggerated humor, misspellings consistent with New York dialectical forms, the aphorism, and especially character types to folklore tradition.

Hamilton Literary Monthly, III (January, 1869)–XL (March, 1906), *passim.* The literary magazine of Shaw's alma mater, Hamilton College; contains numerous important notices of Shaw's activities and accomplishments throughout his career.

HOWE, WILL D. "Early Humorists," *Cambridge History of American Literature.* Vol. II. New York: The Macmillan Co., 1931. Succinct appreciation; emphasizes Shaw as essayist rather than storyteller.

HUDSON, FREDERICK. *Journalism in the United States from 1690-1872.* New York: Harper & Brothers, 1873. Comments on the lack of a system in Shaw's misspellings.

JONES, JOSEPH. "Josh Billings Meets James Marshall," *The Pacific Historical Review,* XIII (December, 1944), 425. Brief account of Shaw's trip west in 1874 and his meeting the man who discovered gold in California.

————. "Josh Billings: Some Yankee Notions on Humor," *Studies in English.* Austin: The University of Texas Press, 1943, pp. 148-61. Highly perceptive view of Shaw's art; emphasizes his unique talents.

————. "Josh Billings Visits a Mark Twain Shrine," *American Notes and Queries,* IV (September, 1944), 83-84. Another view of Shaw's western tour; emphasizes his visit to Twain's old office at the *Virginia City Territorial Enterprise.*

KESTERSON, DAVID B. "Josh Billings and His Burlesque *Allminax,*"

Illinois Quarterly, XXXV (November, 1972), 6-14. Recounts the launching of Shaw's almanac, relates the work to the almanac tradition in America, explores the types of material found in the *Allminax,* and comments on the financial and critical success of the venture.

LANDON, MELVILLE D. *Kings of the Platform and Pulpit.* New York: The Werner Company, 1895. Important picture of Shaw as lecturer by one of his friends.

—————. *Thirty Years of Wit.* New York: The Werner Co., 1899. Contains a brief reminiscence of Shaw.

LANG, ANDREW. *Lost Leaders.* London: Kegan Paul, Trench, Trübner & Co., 1892. Brief, somewhat unappreciative view of Shaw by the renowned British critic.

LEACOCK, STEPHEN. *The Greatest Pages of American Humor.* Garden City, New York: Doubleday, Doran & Co., [1936]. Selections from Shaw's writings; informative biographical headnote.

LUKENS, HENRY CLAY. "American Literary Comedians," *Harper's,* LXXX (April, 1890), 783-97. Brief but laudatory mention of Shaw.

[MASSEY, GERALD]. "Yankee Humor," *Quarterly,* CXXII (January, 1867), 212-37. Favorable glimpse of Shaw's brand of humor and his techniques.

MATTHEWS, BRANDER. "American Humor." *The American of the Future and Other Essays.* New York: Charles Scribner's Sons, 1910. Concludes that Shaw is more of a wit than a humorist.

MEAD, DAVID. *Yankee Eloquence in the Middle West.* East Lansing: Michigan State College Press, 1951. Contains notes on Shaw's successful lecturing in the Middle West.

MELTZER, MILTON. *Mark Twain Himself.* New York: Thomas Y. Crowell Company, 1960. Account of Shaw as lecturer with details of the lyceum system; draws data from Twain's autobiography.

MENCKEN, H. L. *The American Language.* New York: Alfred A. Knopf, 1936. Shaw's innovations in language usage.

MONTAGUE, H., ed. *Wit and Wisdom of Josh Billings.* Winston Salem, North Carolina (privately published), 1913. Random selection from Shaw's works with a praiseful but unreliable introduction.

MOTT, FRANK LUTHER. *A History of American Magazines.* 5 vols. Cambridge: Harvard University Press, 1938. Contains publication data pertinent to Shaw's works.

MUDGE, JAMES. "A Philosophical Humorist," *Methodist Review,* CI (March, 1918), 207-15. Perceptive article portraying Shaw as humorous philosopher having keen insights into life.

MURRELL, WILLIAM. *A History of American Graphic Humor.* 2 vols. New York: The Macmillan Co., 1938. Important information about the illustrators of Shaw's works.

"Neglected Worthies," *Nation,* CVII (August 17, 1918), 165. Appreciative remembrance of Shaw's contributions as humorist on the occasion of the centennial year of his birth.

PAINE, ALBERT BIGELOW. *Mark Twain: A Biography.* 2 vols. New York: Harper and Brothers, 1912. Glimpses of the Shaw-Twain relationship; some general criticism on Shaw.

————. *Th. Nast—His Period and His Pictures.* New York: The Macmillan Co., 1904. Contains insights into the Nast-Shaw relationship; reprints a letter from Shaw to Nast.

PATTEE, FRED LEWIS. *A History of American Literature Since 1870.* New York: The Century Company, 1915. Emphasizes Shaw's mastery of the aphorism.

PLATT, EDMUND. *The Eagle's History of Poughkeepsie.* Poughkeepsie: Platt and Platt, 1905. Reveals many obscure, interesting facts about Shaw's life in Poughkeepsie.

POND, J. B. *Eccentricities of Genius.* New York: G. W. Dillingham Co., 1900. Former acquaintance of Shaw's writes an appreciative sketch of the man, writer, and lecturer.

Selections from the Writings of Josh Billings, or: Proverbial Philosophy of Wit and Humor. Introduction by Carl Purlington Rollins. Athens, Georgia: K. De Renne, 1940. An assortment of Shaw's aphorisms, essays, and miscellaneous pieces; a brief introduction to his life.

SMITH, CHARLES H. (BILL ARP). *The Farm and the Fireside.* Atlanta, Georgia: The Constitution Publishing Co., 1891. Valuable biographical, critical discussion by a friend of Shaw's. Good personal account.

SMITH, FRANCIS SHUBAEL. *Life and Adventures of Josh Billings.* New York: G. W. Carleton & Co., 1883. First biography of Shaw; written by his employer on the *New York Weekly.*

TANDY, JENNETTE. *Crackerbox Philosophers in American Humor and Satire.* New York: Columbia University Press, 1925. Important discussion of Shaw's life and writings—especially the *Allminax*—with a helpful bibliography.

THOMPSON, E. P. "The Home of Josh Billings," *New England Magazine,* n.s. XIX (February, 1899), 696-703. Valuable for its account of Shaw's milieu in Lanesboro, Massachusetts.

[THOMPSON, HAROLD W.]. "Humor." *Literary History of the United States.* New York: The Macmillan Co., [1953], 728-57. A brief survey of Shaw's life and literary contributions, especially the aphorisms and *Allminax*.

TRENT, WILLIAM P. "Retrospect of American Humor," the *Century Magazine*, LXIII (November, 1901), 45-64. Brief summary of Shaw's contributions to American humor.

WEISS, HARRY B. "A Brief History of American Jest Books," *Bulletin of the New York Public Library*, XLVII (April, 1943), 273-89. Contains a brief discussion of *Josh Billings' Trump Kards*.

Index